T0366149

The SUN SHINES after the CLOUDS Have BLOWN AWAY

The SUN SHINES *after the* CLOUDS *Have* BLOWN *AWAY*

BEVERLY ANN CARINUS

*with **Steve Pilkington-Williams***

PARTRIDGE

A Penguin Random House Company

To order additional copies of this book, contact
Toll Free 800 101 2657 (Singapore)
Toll Free 1 800 81 7340 (Malaysia)
orders.singapore@partridgepublishing.com

www.partridgepublishing.com/singapore

Contents

Chapter 1   Beginnings.. 17

Chapter 2   Finding Love... 26

Chapter 3   Devastating News.................................... 33

Chapter 4   Arab Street... 49

Chapter 5   New symptoms.. 60

Chapter 6   Fear and loss.. 68

Chapter 7   Second Radiation and becoming
             a common law wife............................... 75

Chapter 8   Supportive friends.................................. 84

Chapter 9   Vasovagal collapses................................ 101

Chapter 10   Thursdays in Singapore........................ 111

Chapter 11   NO light at the end of the tunnel. 122

Chapter 12   Gaining survival skills........................... 130

Chapter 13   China Town.. 136

Chapter 14   The Operation and wedding................... 149

Chapter 15   Fifty-fifty.. 165

Chapter 16   Coping skills... 182

Chapter 17   Psychedelic becomes reality. 193

Chapter 18   Happiness 202

Chapter 19   Celebrations - Steve turns fifty
and new doors open. 212

Chapter 20   The Hungry ghosts..220

Chapter 21   Cambodia..236

Chapter 22   Travels and Monks...255

Chapter 23   Melt down and finally Acceptance. 268

Dedicated to the memory of our fathers:

Kenneth John Pilkington-Williams

David Bryce Kinsman.

We wish we had been granted more time together.
Always in our hearts.

When you find the light within you
You will know that you have always
Been the center of wisdom.
As you probe deeper into whom you really are
With your lightness and confusion
With your Anger, longings and distortions
You will find your true living soul within you.
Then you will say,
I have known you all my life.
And I have called you many names;
I have called you mother, father, sister, brother and child.
I have called you lover
I have called you sun and flowers.
I have called you my heart.
But never, until this moment;
Called you..........MYSELF.

Based and adapted from a Source Unknown

Acknowledgements

No people real or imaginary were harmed in the writing of this book. This book is based on our story. The facts have been interwoven with our imaginary intimate glimpses into people during their and our profound life changes and daily routines.

To all those very special people out there who have helped form part of our story Thank you!

Special Thanks to

Dr. Judy Wallis for giving me the idea and encouragement to write this book. Thank you for the amazing advice that we received from you when we needed it most.
http://www.RADTeach.com

Grant Clark for making me believe I could and helping guide me through.
http://monkeymagicbook.com

Linda Wilde for being my supportive "IT." You are someone we can always depend on.

Judy Westwater, the founder of The Pegasus children's trust. For being my inspiration and for the guidance and encouragement you gave me in founding www. Rebuildconfidence.webs.com
www.streetkid.org.uk

Prologue

Our story is a love story about two people whose lives ran in parallel lines, although we never met until later in our lives. We both always felt that sense of seeking; looking for that someone who was missing from our lives. Yet once we had experienced the joy of finding each other, fate threw a tragic twist our way.

In 2004 Steve was moving from Dubai to start a new and exciting phase of his life in Singapore. He asked me to join him but just a few months later he fell ill and was diagnosed with an inoperable left based glomus brain-stem tumour.

This story is about our love, Steve's tumour and his determination to live. We were starting our lives together in circumstances very different to what we had planned. We turned what should have been an ending into an exciting new beginning. Steve and I were in a strange country. We were facing and coping with issues that most couples don't have to deal with in a lifetime. It only made our love stronger.

We have learned that an illness such as Steve's brings out the best and the worst behavior from others as they battle with their own level of acceptance. Therefore we have purposely left out any negative content and only write about our own personal experiences.

On this tenth anniversary of our life together we decided to share our story. Little snippets of life in a strange country, living with a brain tumour and our unique love in the hope that it will be of encouragement and inspiration to others suffering hardships.

Steve & Beverly 2014

You know, life fractures us all into little pieces. It harms us, but it's how we glue those fractures back together that make us stronger.

Carrie Jones.

Beverly

Sitting on the plane as it flew out of Durban airport I felt a mixture of emotions. My life had taken me on so many different paths that I felt I had lived many lives in this one lifetime. Deep inside me there had always been an empty space and the feeling that "something was missing from my world".

My heart was sore and heavy because my Grandmother had passed away at the age of ninety four. She had been such a huge influence in my life and the monarch of our family. Due to circumstances her funeral was scheduled to take place on the day my flight was to leave South Africa. I was torn as to whether I should postpone my flight or travel as arranged. My aunt advised me to go. She told me that my Gran's soul was no longer earth bound and on the day of the funeral I would be up in the sky, closer to her than anyone. Looking out of the plane window at the fluffy clouds, I did have the sense that Gran was so close to me and guiding me with her approval because all she ever wanted was for me to be happy.

Two of my grown sons had taken me to the airport and saying goodbye to them and walking away was one of the hardest things I have ever had to do.

At the age of fifty, I was leaving behind all my "security", worldly possessions, family and friends. I packed one suitcase and followed my heart and it felt so right. Steve and I had waited so long for this moment.

I was flying to Singapore to a new life and new adventures. I was about to find myself.

Steve was waiting for me at the airport. He looked so amazingly well. He had always been exceptionally good looking and well-built. He still was despite his recent radiation treatments. I melted into his big blue eyes just as I always had. I had always known that somehow and in some way Steve and I were connected because of the effect those beautiful blue eyes had on me.

I was nervous as I walked up to Steve but he gathered me in his arms with a huge hug and said "welcome Home!" I truly felt for the first time in my life that I was home. My soul had connected with its soul mate. I can never hope to describe that feeling of wholeness. Our life together began in the beautiful garden city of Singapore.

Bev's 50th birthday.

Steve

I watched Bev as she walked through from Immigration towards the baggage reclaim belts at Terminal 2 at Changi Airport at 0600hrs. She looked across through the windows of the Arrivals Hall and our eyes met. She gave me a half nervous smile and a wave, and then waited for her luggage.

The wait seemed endless; it seemed her luggage was last off. When she finally emerged I took her in my arms and felt her body warmth, it felt so good. I took over her luggage trolley and we walked across to the taxi stand. We took a taxi to my condominium and I showed her to our room.

I explained that I had to go to work that day as we had a key strategy meeting. I suggested that perhaps she might like to catch up on some sleep, unpack her luggage and get to know the place.

I felt mixed emotions as I sat in the back of the taxi on my way to the office. I was delighted Bev had finally arrived but I had this sense of nervousness and trepidation as to whether our relationship could survive my tumour. I had just completed my first bout of radiation; forty five minutes a day, five days a week, four weeks in total. I was completely exhausted, with a severe squint in my right eye, lacking co-ordination, experiencing constant severe headaches and nausea, and just a general feeling of being totally out of it.

I could barely take care of myself and it was affecting my self-confidence in a major way. As much as I wanted Bev there, I did not know if we had made the right decision about her moving in as the tumour was going to be major challenge for both of us. All I knew is that I wanted her with me in my life.

Little did I know that her arrival would save me in so many ways!

Chapter One
Beginnings

"Life Begins where fear Ends." **Osho.**

Beverly:

I was born in Dundee Natal South Africa on the 1st August 1954 at 5pm. My mother had told me that I was born exactly at five in the evening, not a minute before or after. She knew this because there had been a radio playing in the delivery room.

The presenter announced that it was 5pm the moment I was born and then he played the song of the Era sung by Nat King Cole; "Smile".

My mother always had a sense of the dramatics. When she was giving birth to my brother, she cried out in agony that she had gone blind because of the pain.

The doctor's response to that was "well, open your bloody eyes then!"

My mother stuck to her fact that I had a birth song and "Smile" was it. Whenever I asked her how she could be so certain of all the details, her response was simply... "Well, I was there wasn't I?" I suppose with that kind of conviction, I adopted my birth song as my philosophy for life. Throughout my life I tend to look at the humorous side of most situations and value the ability to simply smile.

The night before I left South Africa, I received a phone call from my mother. Instead of saying goodbye to me she sang "Smile" in a voice cracking with emotion. Afterwards told me this was her song for me to keep it in my heart wherever I went. So "Smile" did begin my journey of rebirth.

> *"Smile though your heart is aching*
> *Smile even though its breaking*
> ....
> *You'll find that life is still worthwhile*
> *If you just smile."*

I was my parent's first child and my maternal grandmother's first grandchild. My beautiful mother, Ann was just eighteen and my father David was only twenty one at the time of my birth. They were young and in love but they were both impulsive and spontaneous. They were enjoying their young lives to the full. David had come into an inheritance from his parent's estate and they enjoyed spending it and having fun. They were barely able to be responsible for themselves so it must have come as a bit of a shock to find out that they were having a baby.

Their passion was dancing. They did ballroom dancing, jiving and jitterbugging and won many competitions. My mother loved music; her joy was there for all to see. She loved Nat King Cole, Duke Ellington, Eartha Kitt, Buddy Holly and The Ink Spots.

She would hear *"In the mood"* and she would start tapping her feet to the sound until she could contain herself no longer. She would jump up and literally start dancing in the aisles. When music was on she was transported into another world. She had a wardrobe full of dance costumes.

Eighteen months later, my parents provided me with a sister and our perfect family was complete. The first five years of my life were so happy. I remember the laughter and music. There were always parties where parents got together with their children and a good time was had by all. I loved being tossed up into the air and dancing with passion. The children joined the adults in doing "the Hokey Pokey", "Knees up mother brown", "the Charleston" and jiving.

My mother loved books and poetry as well. Each night she would tuck us into bed and recite poetry and read to us. My favourite book was by Lousia May Alcott, "Little Women".

"The Diary of Iris Vaughan" became a family classic and there was much laughter as we asked for the "funny bits" to be read again and again. My mother installed in me the love and respect I have for books and all things written. I grew up reading every Enid Blyton book that was available. I loved the famous five mysteries and got lost in the romantic world of Gypsies.

After story time, my mother would kneel with us next to our beds and we would give thanks for the day. My level of confidence was so strong then that I even changed the words of a prayer to suit myself.

I was told to recite "pity my simplicity" but this made no sense to me so I used my own words "Pretty mice and pretty me!"

No amount of persuasion could get me to use any other words but my own.

I was so secure that I did not pick up on any of the "undercurrents" occurring in the adults lives around me. There had been a lot happening while I was locked in my protective little world. My maternal grandparents had moved to Livingstone in Northern Rhodesia. My mother had been exceptionally close to her father and wanted to be near him. So Ann and David decided to follow them.

We lived near my Grandparents. The love my Grandmother had for me was enormous and continued throughout my life even though we lived apart for many years. In those formative years of my life she played a huge role in getting me to believe in myself. She always called me "Princess".

When I told other children I was a Princess, they chanted back at me "No you are not!"

On telling my Gran this she confronted the children and told them that I was a Real Princess, I was her Princess!" So for a while I did believe that I was a real Princess.

She also called me "Angel Face". One day my mother, my gran and I were in town. I saw a doll that I wanted. I asked my mother for it and she said no. So I threw a temper tantrum and appealed to my Gran. She was trying to appease me and calling me "Angel Face".

A man passing by said "she has the cheek to call her angel face?"

My Gran was the epitome of "dynamite comes in small packages". She was tiny and wore small size three shoes that she had made especially in Italy. She could stand her ground! She had an eccentric, engaging personality that made people love her no matter how outrageous she might be.

I started school at Blue Gum lane in Livingstone. I enjoyed going to school and was very confident. In my first year there the Queen arrived for a visit to Livingston. I was one of the many children who lined the airport. We wore our school uniforms and waved small hand held British flags. We waved with frenzy hoping to be noticed by the Queen.

Little did I know then that my soul mate had been born. He would be the person who would heal my heart and who would be able to take all the little pieces of my fractured life and glue them together. It would take a lifetime to find him.

It was the start of all the "coincidences" that shaped our lives. We were always so close yet so far apart. When I was three years old, Steve was born in Ladysmith, Natal, South Africa, just sixty nine kilometers from my birthplace of Dundee.

Steve and his father.

Steve:

I was born in Ladysmith, Natal at 0345hrs on the 21st February 1958. Years later I asked my mother how she was so sure of the time. She told me she could never forget the relief after nine hours of labour. She thrived on drama, so I'm sure the doctors and nursing staff were very relieved when she was discharged and took me home.

Home at that time was a two-bedroomed apartment on the main street in Ladysmith, a small farming town. Its sole claim to fame was that it was the Natal head-quarters of the British Forces in the Second Boer War.

My father Kenneth was a sales rep with the Rothmans Cigarette Company. In those days it was a prestigious and well-paying position. It took him away from home for days every week, which must have been difficult for my mother. She was twenty one years old, from a large Irish Catholic

English-speaking family living in Port Elizabeth, and now stuck in an Afrikaans-speaking farming town where "rooinekke" were not exactly welcome.

We moved from town to town and city to city as Rothmans decreed and as my father rapidly climbed the corporate ladder. At a young age he was appointed General Manager of Rothmans Southern Rhodesia and so we moved to Salisbury. My earliest memories are from this time, playing cowboys in our large garden and spending hours climbing the massive avocado tree that dominated the front garden.

When I was four my mother came home from hospital with my new baby sister. I was not amused as I had wanted a horse. I decided it was time to leave, so with my cowboy outfit on and my dog Mr. Jinks at my side we hit the road. The police picked us up four hours later outside the Salisbury Showgrounds. Mr. Jinks and I were not happy, even though the police officers thought it quite funny.

My father travelled a lot, and he took me with him on several trips. We would fly in magnificent Viscounts to Lusaka, Nairobi, Kampala and Lilongwe. He would leave me with his reps families during the day and we stayed in great old colonial hotels at night. My father was my super-hero.

We moved to a new large home in Arcturus Road on the other side of town, and close to my new school, St. Michaels. The new house was ideal for entertaining, and due to my father's position he had to. There were regular big parties on Saturday nights which my mother loved as she was a total extrovert, as opposed to my father's quiet nature. My father's mother had passed away when he was five years old, and he was brought up by his sister Joan whom he idolized.

I remember getting up to use the bathroom during one of my parents' parties and finding my father sitting in the bedroom passage in front of a built-in cupboard. He was assisting our cat Chookie give birth to a litter of kittens whilst my mother was dancing and singing meters away in the lounge. That was my father, and that was my mother.

We continued to move as my father's career took off. When I was eight we ended up living in Cape Town up against the back of Table Mountain in the suburb of Newlands. It was paradise for a youngster. My playground was the forests of the mountain. My group of friends in our small suburb built forts in the trees; explored long-abandoned mansions set in the forests, drank mountain water from the many streams, and ate bush pigeon that we shot with our catapults and air guns.

On summer evenings after work my father would pack us into his car and we would drive the twenty minutes over the neck down to Hout Bay beach where we would have a beach picnic in between playing in the surf and chasing the flocks of seagulls with my dog Rusty. Life was great!

CHAPTER TWO
Finding Love

Being deeply loved by someone gives you strength,
while loving someone deeply gives you courage
- Lao Tzu

Beverly:

Steve and I had met many years previously after being introduced by a mutual friend. We had the same interests and would often meet to talk as well as email each other about our lives. Back then Steve and I were only friends but so many people had put us "together" romantically and yet we weren't. It is strange how others could see the chemistry between us long before we were aware of it. Due to circumstances in our lives Steve moved to a different city and we stopped communicating. I think that our feelings for each other were becoming strong and rather than hurt anyone we just did not communicate for three years. I often thought of Steve and wondered if he was doing well. I just thought that our friendship was not meant to be and felt a huge sense of loss. It was during this period that I travelled a lot to the England and America. I spent several beautiful summers in England.

My life has always prepared me for the next step. Once again, many "coincidences" began to occur that shaped what was to come. My children had all long left home so I had time to myself. I was wondering just what to do with it, when one day I saw an advert for a Hospice Caregivers course. I joined it and thrived on the study.

I went onto become a caregiver and later a bereavement counselor for Hospice. It was often tough sad work. I was helping the dying to come to terms with death and counselling the family for a year afterwards but I was helping people to get over loss and giving them skills to rebuild their lives. I spoke with doctors, nurses, always eager to learn more. I did learn a great deal about dealing with illness and suffering as well as medication and how to look after myself as a care giver too. I began specializing in bereavement care for children. During this period I studied and obtained a developmental psychologist certificate to enable me to so. I was active and fulfilled in my role as a bereavement worker.

Unknown to me at this time Steve was also travelling and developing his career. We had both got divorced without knowing that each of us had separated from our partners. One evening Steve called me out of the blue. He was living in Dubai and so we began our correspondence. It was almost daily, writing about the happenings in our everyday life and then our feelings for each other slowly and cautiously coming through the mails.

We would often plan to meet but due to Steve's business commitments and travels, our plans were always blocked. Once, I was traveling to London and Steve planned to meet me there. He knew from my mails how I came alive in London and wanted to share that special feeling with me. It didn't happen, the first Gulf War erupted and Steve was stuck out on an oil rig for weeks. We wrote to each other for three years and in those three years met once a year each year. The first time Steve hugged me it was like an electrical bolt going through me. It was the most amazing feeling in the entire world and I never ever wanted that hug to end. He wrote to me that the hug had the same effect on him and he had a serious problem pulling out of it.

My friends were growing increasingly frustrated with me. None of them had ever seen Steve and jokingly they said they thought he was just a figment of my imagination. I was beginning to wonder too, if I just had conjured him up; a divinely gorgeous apparition that I only had the power to hold onto for a few very precious moments, before he disappeared into the horizon again.

Friends tried, they really did, to set me up with someone "real". On one occasion a friend invited me to her house warming party. I was also doing a bit of catering for party functions and so I offered to do the catering for her party. As soon as I arriving I immediately noticed she had invited some "eligible gentlemen" along to introduce me to. I was not interested at all and spent most of the evening nursing a glass of wine while looking out at the beautiful ocean views.

A man did venture up to me and began the conversation: "So how long have you been divorced then?"

I felt indignant, what a personal question to ask a complete stranger. I excused myself from the conversation and decided that this was no fun, I wanted to go home. I passed by the kitchen where a group of men were standing around swigging their beers. I overheard them talking about...me.

One man was telling the others; "She's the type of woman you should go for. She's a looker, her children are grown up and live outside the home, she owns her house and she can cook!"

I walked into the kitchen pretending I had not heard the conversation and said goodbye where upon one of the men said "Oh, let me give you a lift home."

I smiled sweetly and replied, "No need thank you, you forgot to mention I own a car too!"

My youngest son was also protective of me. One evening I went out for a quick supper with a male friend of a friend. I had been counseling him on his relationship with the woman he adored so it wasn't a date just two people needing some food. We were sitting having dinner opposite each other in a booth at a steak house and he started to laugh. He told me not to turn around but at the very next booth sitting back to back with me was my son.

He was doing his "protection". I pretended not to see him but as I left the restaurant, I mentioned to the staff that the young man in the booth was my son. I told them it was his birthday. I had the last laugh because as I walked out I looked back to see my son looking embarrassed. His table was surrounded by the staff holding a lit sparkler above his head and singing and clapping in union to "Happy birthday!"

Nothing and no-one could match or even come close to the kind of communication that Steve and I shared. I didn't want to waste any more time. I knew that I had found what I was seeking all my life but it just seemed so impossible and improperly that we would ever be together.

The universe was taking another step in preparing my future though. I started doing belly dancing classes along with a group of middle aged women. We started doing it to keep fit but they decided to work towards putting on a concert in the town hall. By that time it was ready to be staged I was on my way to Singapore and mercifully missed being in the concert. The morning and evening classes we practiced at were full of laughter and the dancing itself was therapeutic and uplifting.

Then the news from Steve, his life was turning around. He had got a new job in Singapore. He said he would love for me to join him in his new adventure and what "will be, will be." I felt so excited and alive. I was visiting my niece in London and then going to visit my son in America and then back to London before I flew back to South Africa. We decided I would fly to Singapore once Steve had got himself settled. I was so ecstatically happy. At last our lives were merging together and we were both looking forward to the exciting new developments. Steve had written to me that he was finding life so exciting and felt as if he was embarking on a whole new life pattern. He said it was about time that he and I were given a break in life. He felt that it was his year for doing what he always wanted to do and asked me to share it with him. Steve sent me a message that said;

> *"Come with me*
> *To a quiet place*
> *Where Sun and breeze and grass*
> *Erase troubles, conflicts and senseless chatter.*
> *Come with me to find*
> *What matters most....*
> *Holding you*
> *I find my heaven close."*

We were planning ahead for a new life and a new start. We had known for a long time that together we not only had a strong love but the ability to erase the hurts from our past.

Extracts from Steve's mails to me.

"I remember a wonderful quote I once read from a Spanish poet, Juan Ramo'n Jime'nez - *"if they give you ruled paper, write the other way."* I seem to have lived my life according to my own rules. The most impressive photo I have ever seen of you, that epitomizes my thought pattern here, is that wonderful one of you as a definite 16 year old, giving the camera the once over. There was amazing spirit shown in that photo! I wish I could have known that girl at 16 – who knows what could have happened? It's never too late to dream. I am finding life so exciting at present; I feel I am embarking on a whole new life pattern. It's time you and I were given a break in life."

"Thanks so much for the photo I love it! There is just so much self-confidence and yessss attitude to it. It really is amazing. I wish we could be young again and meet at that level. I promise you if I had been present when that photo was taken you wouldn't have stood a chance."

"I have just got home and am listening to the lighthouse Family with a glass of wine. My favourite right now is *"I wish I Knew How It felt to be free."* Wow, to be totally free how wonderful! As I mentioned in a previous mail, this is my year for doing things I have always wanted to do. Share it with me?"

CHAPTER THREE

Devastating News

We must let go of the life we planned so as to accept the one that is waiting for us -

Joseph Campbell.

Beverly:

I had returned to London from America and in a few days' time I would be back home in South Africa and begin making arrangements to join Steve in Singapore. I was still in London when I received **the** call from Steve, a horrid moment frozen in time. Steve told me that he had just been diagnosed with a rare Glomus Brain stem tumour and that the ENT Specialist in Dubai had wanted to operate immediately. Steve was called aside by one of the staff and told he should not have the operation. They suggested that he rather seek a second opinion and treatment in Singapore. Steve was making arrangements to fly to Singapore as soon as possible.

How does the mind deal with news like that? Fear was the first thing that grabbed my heart. There were just so many thoughts in that one second before replying.

What can one say? What can one do? I cannot even remember what I said to Steve as the shock shut my brain down.

After the call I lay crying for hours. I cried for Steve and for myself. I had my hospice training so I was left in no doubts about the seriousness of the tumour and all the consequences. What made it even worse was that a friend of mine had just lost her husband to a brain tumour and I had counselled her through it. I had too much knowledge that I didn't want right then.

The Five stages of grief appear over days, weeks, months or years after hearing bad news but they all hit me with a massive impact once I had put down the phone.

Denial and isolation: There has been a mistake! NOT Steve, he has always been so extra fit and healthy. This can't be happening to us! I was blocking out the words and facts that were screaming in my head in order not to deal with the pain.

Anger: I was so angry - so very angry at the universe and life. WHY? Why was this happening to Steve? Life was not fair! Why now when we were planning to start a future together?

Bargaining: Oh please, don't let this be true. Let it all be a mistake and I promise I will be the best person ever! I was trying to think of the best deal I could give the universe in order to reverse the situation.

Depression: A great sadness settled over me and I felt totally overwhelmed by it. I knew no amount of tears could make it better.

Acceptance: Ok, Beverly, this has happened. All your life you have called on your reserves of strength to get through, do it again. What can you do about the situation? Be strong, you fight it! Find the strength for both yourself and Steve!

I kept thinking if I felt this way Steve must be totally crushed and devastated at the news. He had taken it in a matter of fact way saying "these things happen in life." He appeared calm and in control but I knew he must be going through such a very difficult time. I knew he too would have to work through the five stages of grief and come to terms with it in his own way.

When Steve arrived in Singapore, it was confirmed that it was a rare inoperable left- sided Glomus brain stem tumour. For a time it was thought there were two tumours. It was actually one that had moved through a narrow cavity and pushed through to the other side so it was one bar- bell shaped tumour. Steve told me that given the fact that he had a brain tumour he no longer expected me to join him in Singapore. I told him I was still going to join him, there were no doubts in my mind at all about that.

When Steve was diagnosed the only option the doctor gave him was to have immediate radiation treatment. He was told that he would not have survived an operation to remove the tumour. We had decided that Steve would have his first four weeks of radiation treatment before I joined him. Steve wanted it that way; he had always been so independent, strong, healthy and resourceful. He didn't want anyone to see him in any other way. He began his first bout of radiation totally alone and isolated in a foreign country.

The isolation I felt back in South Africa was awful. It was dreadful not to be with Steve and not to hear about the developments first hand. It was frustrating not being able to help him in the way that Hospice had trained me to. I would get late night calls from Steve; he would be totally confused and would often fall. Along with his eye sight, all his motor coordination skills were out. He was bumping into and falling over things.

Steve had no medical insurance or coverage as he had just started his new job so he had to go straight from radiation treatments back to work - unheard of! He had the most amazing ability to just get himself through that treatment on his own with no one around to help or assist him. He had a maid Natty who came to clean the house once a week and an old Chinese man, Richard. He would call Richard and order groceries which he would deliver to the apartment. Other than that there was no-one to assist. Once I had moved in with Steve I heard from the maid Natty, how she would have to wash blood off the stairs where he had so often fallen.

We much later found out that Steve had chosen the wrong neurosurgeon and that the levels of radiation that had been given to him that first time were way too high. Because of the urgency to treat the tumour there was no time to go for other opinions. Steve had been so very lucky that the doctor in Dubai who was an ENT specialist did not operate to remove the tumour as he wanted to because if he had Steve would certainly have died.

Those two months were very tough on Steve. It still amazes me that Steve found the inner strength and resolution to get through that period on his own and maintain his job, which involved a lot of travel. In fact straight after the first bout of radiation treatments, Steve had to travel to an oil and gas conference in Houston in the USA. The conference came straight after the end of his four weeks of radiation treatment and so we decided that I would join Steve in Singapore once he got back from America. We wasted no time, Steve arrived back in Singapore on a Friday night and he was at the airport the next morning to meet my arrival in Singapore.

We knew we had exactly three weeks before the start of Steve's next treatment. I had last seen Steve a year before when he had visited me in South Africa on his way back to Dubai. I suppose with most long distant relationships there is an awkward moment of getting to know each other beyond just verbal and written communication yet Steve and I just fell into life side by side as if it was the most natural thing in the world. It felt as if we had always been together. We did not have the pressure of wondering if the next few weeks would make or break our relationship as it was just the easiest and natural progression and felt so right and good. We had found each other and felt whole, united and very calm.

Strangely enough we did not discuss the tumour or the impact it would have on our lives. We jokingly called it our "probation" time as were getting to know each other and enjoy the time we had. Our favourite place to go for supper was a little Italian restaurant situated right on the beach. We would sit with our bare feet in the sand, a guitar player singing in the background. We would spend many happy hours there just talking and talking into the early hours of the morning.

Steve had finished a harrowing course of radiation treatments and was about to embark on his second. We could not plan our future ahead as there were so many medical uncertainties. We knew that our love made us stronger and we would get through any situation as long as we had each other. There is never any guarantee in life about how long you and your partner will be granted together but when you live under the constant threat of an unstable tumour, things become so much more magnified. Every second of every day becomes a precious moment in time.

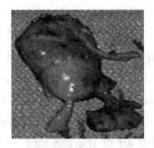

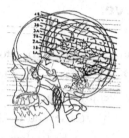

A Glomus tumour Similar to the mass growing inside Steve's brain.

Steve's neurologist diagnose of where the tumour is situated.

Clinical Notes: Glomus tumour.

Technique: Whole brain sagittal T1, axial T2, FLAIR and post contrast axial and coronal T1 scans performed. In addition, thin axial T1 and T2 and post contrast

Findings:

There is an infiltrating mass, with multiple areas of low signal consistent with flow voids, centred on the left side of the base of skull in the jugular foramen. It infiltrates medially into the right petrous apex and right side of the clivus, laterally into the mastoid and middle ear and superiorly lies adjacent to the left Meckle's cave. It extends posteriorly into the left side of the pre pontine cistern and is in contact with the left side of the pons. Inferiorly and contiguous with the main mass, it extends into the carotid space with anterior displacement of the left ICA. The left sigmoid sinus appears thickened and heterogeneous in signal indicating extension of the glomus tumour into the sinus. The proximal left jugular vein is likely to be occluded. Maximal trans axial dimensions of the mass are 3.7 x 1.8cm. No previous imaging is available for comparison.

Report on the Glomus Tumour.

Steve in good health

Steve:

I had left South Africa to open a branch of our company in Dubai. I was looking forward to the challenge as I had always enjoyed starting and building up new companies. It was only after several weeks in Dubai that I realized what a challenge I had taken on with all of the red tape and bureaucracy involved. It was trying on one's patience but within a short time we were up and running.

I was travelling throughout the Middle East and South-East Asia regularly, but really felt an affinity for Asia and decided that I would move there eventually. I was travelling back to South Africa every year as well and always visited Bev. The visits were always short but also very therapeutic as I felt this incredible connection to her.

Back in Dubai I was approached by a Head-Hunter on behalf of an international logistics company in Singapore. He wanted me to join them on a two year contract, to start an oil and gas vertical for them in Asia. I knew nothing about logistics but I was an oil and gas man who wanted to get to Asia. I went and spoke to our MD about it and told him I had wanted to move to Singapore for a while, so was it not possible for the company to open up an office out there as I enjoyed the company and did not really want to leave them. It was discussed at Board level, but they thought the timing was not quite right and so I accepted the new position and resigned from my old company. About five years later they contacted me to open up for them in Asia, but by that time it was too late.

Whilst serving my notice period and planning my move I noticed slight issues with my eyesight when watching TV in the evenings. At first I thought it may be the angle I was watching from, so kept adjusting my position, but it just kept getting worse. One morning on the way to work it was so bad that I stopped in at an optician and had a check on my eyes. He told me he had to prescribe new lenses as my astigmatism was not suitable for my current lenses.

I went back two days later to pick up my new glasses. I could not see anything in focus so he retested me and said these were the correct lenses. I told him he was hopeless, but he said there was something wrong that he could not fix and that I needed to see an ophthalmologist. I took my weekend on a Friday and Saturday, as did most people in Dubai but by Sunday morning my right eye had pulled in towards my nose and I was squint and could not drive. I opened the phone book and looked up ophthalmologist. I found what appeared to be a South African sounding name. I called, and sure enough, she was from Pretoria, so I booked an appointment on the spot and caught a taxi in.

She examined my eyes and asked to be excused for a minute. She came back with a young Canadian colleague of hers whom she introduced and explained that if his diagnosis confirmed what she thought my problem was she would have to hand me over to him as this was his area of expertise. Strange I thought.

He was extremely friendly and professional and went straight in with a series of tests. After quite a while he sat in front of me and explained that my condition appeared to be caused by pressure on my optical nerves and wanted to refer me for both a CT and MRI scan just to check. In the interim he managed to obtain a plinth which he put in my glasses to ensure that, whilst I still could not drive, at least I could walk vaguely straight and did not have to walk around with one eye shut and close to walls and railings to ensure I did not fall over or bump into people.

I registered at the hospital and went straight in for my scans. After a while of waiting, I was called in by the Chief Radiologist who told me I had a brain tumour and needed an operation as soon as possible to remove it. He calmly stated that the resident Saudi Arabian brain surgeon was on vacation, but his colleague, an ENT from Syria would perform the surgery. With that he got up, told me to wait, and the ENT would be with me shortly. On meeting the ENT I decided there was no ways he would do anything to me. He was bouncing around like a hyperactive kid with about ten cups of coffee in him. I politely told him I needed to have a think about it and would come back to him shortly.

I walked out of the consulting room and sat on a chair in the passage. I was approached by the receptionist who explained to me that there was something serious about my tumour. She said that although it was very unethical, there was someone I should have a quick conversation with. She told me to go to the hospital coffee shop and that this person would meet me there. I was intrigued so duly went there and waited.

A person I had seen in the X-ray department came and asked if he could join me. He sat and explained that what he was doing was highly unethical but he had to explain the seriousness of my situation, and what my options were. He was an experienced radiologist from Singapore who was doing a locum in Dubai and it turned out he had been looking at my scans with the Chief Radiologist. There was apparently much excitement in the department as they, apart from the locum, had never seen a tumour like mine. He explained that he had come across a similar tumour in a patient only once in his ten years' experience in Singapore and that not one neurosurgeon there would even attempt to remove it as it was a 99.9% chance the procedure would either kill the patient or at best leave them seriously debilitated. I thanked him for his advice and asked what he would do if he was in my situation. He recommended a neurosurgeon he had worked with in Singapore, gave me his contact numbers, and left.

All my life I had had to cope with situations that I had to sort out myself, so I had no time to sit and think "Why me, why now?" I had to get on with this and fix it – now. Twenty four hours later I flew out of Dubai to Singapore, arriving on a Thursday morning.

On the day of my arrival I had an appointment with Dr. Nasty – apparently one of Singapore's pre-eminent Neurosurgeons. He carried out a series of "tests" on me, mainly consisting of holding his hands out to sides, clicking his fingers and asking if I could hear them, then holding a pencil in front of me and telling me to follow it with my eyes without moving my head. He then told me to go and have a CT and MRI scan and we would take it from them. I had the same tests done to me by so many doctors over the next ten years.

I waited until the scan results came out and had a consultation with Dr. HK – the hospital's Chief Radiologist. He informed me it was a very aggressive glomus tumour that required immediate treatment. He told me he would discuss it with Dr. Nasty but that I had to start my treatment the next Monday, but that I needed to be fitted out with my mask immediately. Dr. HK told me that my tumour was extremely rare and that it was only the third one he had come across in twenty five years of practice.

My sister was living in Singapore at the time and I was staying with her until she left in a few weeks' time for Chicago where her company had transferred her to. I went back to her apartment and sat on her roof-top deck looking out to sea thinking to myself "What the heck is going on"?

I had a sleepless night. It was the first time I had really had time to think "what is this all about?"

I went into my new company the next morning to start work. I had kept them up to date on everything as it was all happening, but had requested a face-to-face meeting with the President – Asia (RP), just to let him know exactly what the situation was.

He listened politely and asked one question, "Can you do the job?"

I replied I could and he called in his PA and instructed her to take me down to my office. I started work there and then.

Treatment started on the Monday at 1200hrs. For five days a week for four weeks I would go into the office early to get the hours in, catch a taxi to the hospital at 1130hrs and go down the cancer center to report for treatment. I would climb onto the table and wait for mask to be fitted. This mask had catches on the sides which were locked into place with a brace on the treatment bed to ensure I could not move my head during the treatment and end up frying healthy tissue. Once the mask was fitted and we were all ready the music would start and the treatment would begin.

I would always ask how long todays' treatment would be and they would tell me. I had worked as a commercial diver for seven years after finishing my studies and used to count down the time to go in my head during my decompression stops whilst waiting to surface. I did this mainly out of a way to pass the time and to see how accurate my sense of timing was as most of our work at that time was in either nil visibility or murky water where there was no sea-life to watch whilst we waited. It's funny how small things like counting down the time during my treatment helped, and I was always pleased when I could ask the nurses "Why did we have five minutes extra today?"

I would the go to the washroom, adjust my tie and the get a taxi back to the office and carry on working. One day my PA said to me on my return from hospital "You are very red today". Yes – I suppose with that amount of radiation in my head I would be.

When I first started my treatments I found it strange watching patients before me come out of the radiation room and heading for the washroom where I could hear them throwing up. I wondered what that was all about. The worst part of waiting was seeing the children coming in. Some would be completely washed out and barely able to look up whilst they waited patiently for their turn. One young girl of about nine years old used to be wheeled in screaming and trying to escape her wheelchair with her mother and a nursing sister holding her down. On one occasion she was struggling so much she urinated and I looked across at her father, a few tears running down his face as a pool of urine gathered beneath her. I could only imagine what he was going through must be worst any parent could.

I was extremely fit when I started that first treatment. For years I had exercised six days a week whenever possible. I usually did forty five minutes weights followed by a minimum forty five minutes cardio. I also have an extremely high pain threshold, but nothing prepared me for the side effects of the treatments. The intense headaches started the first night following treatment. The intensity of it was immense and it seemed to actually be moving around in my head like a worm; first in the right side temple, then on to the left side back of my head. It was continuously moving. Then the muscle cramps and spasms started. With all of these side effects kicking in I could not sleep, despite taking strong sleeping pills.

I would wake up in the mornings totally drained and drag myself off to work, then a treatment, back to work, home, collapse on the couch, unable to move due to the headaches and muscle cramps. I had issues with my balance and started slipping and falling on the stairs in the apartment, sometimes leaving a trail of blood on the bannister or walls.

Dr. Nasty had me on large doses of medication; Firstly the cortico-steroids, which caused my head to swell up, pain-killers, tablets for this, these pills for that. For a person adverse to medications this was rather unpleasant and I started having reactions to some of the medications.

It was difficult for me to explain what was going on to Bev, so I always tried to sound as upbeat as I could when we spoke or I emailed her. After all, I was going to be fine again after this treatment and she could join me – the "old" Steve we both remembered. I did not realize at the time, but looking back at it years later, I had started one the first of the five steps – Denial and Isolation. I was already thinking that everything would be fine after this treatment, but for the time being I was on a own, just lying in my dark bedroom over weekends, wishing the head and body aches would go away – forever.

My two mainstays of support, besides Bev back in South Africa, during this time were my twice weekly char Natty. She would wash and clean the mess I left all over the apartment and Richard the grocery delivery man. I would phone in my order and Richard would deliver it in his little van that evening. Richard was an elderly man whose strength was fading so we had a kind of relay going for delivery. Richard would unload the boxes from his van in the basement car-park, carry them half way up the stairs where he would leave them and I would stumble down and take them up to the kitchen. We would then both sit worn out by the effort halfway up the stairs whilst I made out his cheque, both of us tired out in our own way.

CHAPTER FOUR

Arab Street

Enlightenment means waking up to what you truly are and then being that.

Adyashanti

Arab Street

The Arabian life style is seen in Arab Street. It has one of the largest mosques in Singapore, The Sultan mosque and the calls to prayer vibrate from it. The roads are filled with colourful two storied wooden shuttered shop houses. These shops sell ethnic Arabian goods; jewelry, Persian carpets; rattan and basket ware, spices, flowers, sheesha pipes, prayer mats, fabrics and eastern clothing. Shopping here, you are invited to bargain the price of the goods. There are many money changers along the route. There are belly dancing studios and costume rental shops. It's a hive and buzz of activity as men and women clad in traditional Arabian dress go about their day. There are many restaurants and food courts all serving traditional Arabian foods, Arabian coffee and sheesha. The air has a heady smell of sweet perfume, coffee and rich spices.

Everyone loves to eat in Singapore. The favourite form of greeting is "Have you had lunch?"

Beverly:

Steve was working at his new job which was very demanding and involved a lot of travel. He also had a temperamental Regional President who was also very demanding. It hurt me so much to see Steve treated in such a disrespectful way. The RP had seemed like such a wonderful and genuine person. Steve had told him about his tumour and he employed Steve with the full facts of it. The tumour was deemed a preexisting illness so he could not offer a company medical scheme to Steve yet he promised that he would look into getting medical assistance for Steve. Once Steve started the radiation treatments though, he had no compassion. Steve would go for radiation dressed in his collar and tie for work and go from there straight to work to do a full day's work. He often had to change his appointments for radiation to suit his work travel commitments.

We knew that the first series of radiation treatments had not worked. The tumour had not reduced in fact it had shown a slight growth. I wondered how much longer Steve would be able to work and the future financial consequences were really scary to think about. I started to look for some kind of work to do myself. Steve had a work pass but in Singapore if you lose the work position that is stated on the work pass, you need either find another position or leave the country within thirty days. I was only in Singapore on a holiday pass which only allowed me to stay in the country for thirty days.

While Steve went to work I would explore Singapore taking in the sights and sounds of this beautiful city. While walking the streets of Singapore and exploring the variety of cultures and areas, I found myself on Arab Street. Beautiful shop houses painted brightly in a variety of colours, making the street look so vibrant and alive. All the shops display exotic silk fabrics and many Persian carpets. The shops all sell very similar ware and mostly with "for sale" sign in their window displays; I wondered how they all manage to do business. Most of the shops have stock that spills over onto the pavement areas, as you walk through Arab Street you walk between the shops and their outside displays. Narrow spaces for walking and shop owners calling out to you to have a look.

I stopped outside a shop; it was painted bright pink and blue. It sold belly dancing costumes so intrigued I was drawn inside. There were row upon row of belly dancing costumes all exquisitely tailored and in so many different styles and colours. I spent a long time just looking through them and finally found a costume I really wanted. Rich Egyptian music was played loudly in the shop and the catchy DD tlt Dtkt DD tkt Dtkt tk rhythms made me feel like dancing.

The owner, Lillian seeing my enchantment with the shop came over to talk to me. Before saying hello she first asked me if I have had lunch and I replied "Yes, thank you."

I only found out later from experience that "Have you had lunch?" is a formal polite greeting that most Singaporeans use.

If you reply, "No, I have not had lunch yet." it places them in a difficult position of feeding you something for lunch. It took me a while to understand this and I wondered why when I replied that I had not had lunch yet, I would be given food, even a banana anything that was available. So the polite reply is "Yes, I have had lunch thank you."

We sat down in her shop and we began to talk. She invited me to join her for tea. Lillian sent Joy, her maid from the Philippines to fetch us tea. I sat in polite conversation awaiting my cup of tea to arrive and expecting the traditional tea pot, cups and saucers. What arrived were two massive pull string plastic bags filled to the top with chai, a sticky sweet spicy milky tea. The top of the bag was drawn together and a straw had been inserted in the top of it. I was handed the bag of hot tea. I did not know what to do with it and my mind was thinking quickly." How was I ever going to drink this amount of tea in one sitting? How could I hold it all the time and not drip it or spill it?" I watched Lillian as she sipped hers and then hung it on the armrest of the couch we were sitting on. I did the same.

The tea bag!

Arab street lunch

As we chatted Lilian confided in me that she had a medical problem and I was able to give her the advice she needed due to my Hospice experience. She was very grateful and invited me to a Belly dancing evening at her studio.

She took me upstairs to her dance studio. We climbed barefoot up a steep narrow staircase. The entrance to the studio was from the front road. In Arab Street, everyone took off their shoes and left them on the pavement outside the shop before entering the shops bare foot. I always found this amazing as having come from Africa, where any shoes left outside would disappear immediately. There were always a pile of shoes outside the shop entrances and they were still there when you came out.

The studio was like a scene from Arabian nights! There was a huge full length mirror on the one wall, which stretched the full length of the room. The walls were covered with bright colourful silks and the room had Arabian lanterns and

Sheesha pipes adoring it. Heady incense filled the air. The lighting was soft and seductive.

The evening function was a "dress up" event and so I arrived in my newly bought belly dancing costume. I entered the studio to a fusion of bright colours as all the women's rainbow coloured costumes blended with the silk curtains. The women all welcomed me and I joined them sitting on the floor and then the music began. Everyone jumped up pulling me along with them and began dancing and gliding along to the Egyptian beat: the fast pace of the DD tkt Dtkt tk, DD tkt Dtkt tk rhythm. The trancelike beat DmtDt DmtDt and the sensual Dtt tt DD tm D tt tt DDtm "the dance of the veils" rhythm. To honour the fact that I was visiting them from Africa, a belly dancing teacher, Caroline who was from another studio, put on an African drum beat music and did a fusion of Arabic and African dance. Once she had completed her dance, all the women got up and with much laughter and abandon we dance together to the sound of Africa!

I visited the shop again a few days later. Lillian knew that I was looking for a place to do my counselling work from so she offered me a small empty area upstairs. It was next to her stock room and outside a second dance studio she had. The narrow stair case was often full of stock for the shop that my clients would have to climb over. The little area outside the studio was indeed little. It only had enough room for a table with a chair on either side one for me and one for my client. I hung the walls in the same brightly coloured silks as the dance studio and I had a curtain partition that I could close. Behind the client was a window with brightly painted wooden shutters that I could open. It overlooked the inner small court yard. I felt like a bohemian gypsy.

Lillian said my business would attract customers into her shop and that until I was established there was no need for me to pay rental. A poster with a photograph of me was made offering my counselling services and it was put into the shop window. I had yet to establish a cliental base so I went into the shop on most days to be able to counsel "walk in" clients.

My days of "Arabian nights" in Singapore began with dance. Each morning I would join Lillian's dance class. It was a wonderful way to start the day feeling so energized and alive. My little consulting room upstairs was filling up quickly with Clients who were becoming regular. We could start taking booking which was much better for me as I no longer had to sit in the shop waiting for walk in clients. I would join in a late afternoon dancing class too before I made my way home. Lillian was teaching dance and also preforming at functions and so she began training me to take classes for her whenever she was not available. The dance was wonderful therapy for me where I could just forget everything and be in the moment.

The maid Joy became a dear friend and we shared many laughs together. She would have loved to dance if she had been given the opportunity. Often along with the music in the shop there would be a video playing of belly dancing, so she had easily picked up all the moves. Whenever Lillian was out of the shop and there were no shoppers, we would dance along to the belly dancing videos, "D DD tlt Dtkt DD tkt Dtkt tk!" Laughing together and feeling the joy of dance.

Maids in Singapore.

Most Singapore homes have maids. Almost all the housing has a maid's room built in near the kitchen area, where the foreign maids who are bought into the country will live. There are not many rules to protect them and they work for their employers full time, very often not even getting a day off. Singapore maids are also known as domestic helpers; "ah-mahs" The monthly salary for a maid is usually SGD 350 although sometimes it is much less than this. The maids come from neighboring countries such as Indonesia and the Philippines. They are very poor and work to send back money to their families each month. Often they have to pay back their airfare to either to the agency who employed them or their employers before they can start earning the money for themselves.

Joy was earning a lot less than the suggested salary and she worked twenty four hours a day. She would begin her day by making breakfast for Lillian and then cleaning their apartment. She would catch the MRT (Mass Rapid Transit) to

Arab Street and clean the shop thoroughly before opening it. Her next task would be to serve the customers who came into the shop. Throughout the day she would be sent on errands to fetch tea and lunch. She was not allowed to be seen doing nothing. Then it was home in the evenings to cook supper for Lillian and do the washing and ironing. She had no time off and no private life at all. She was one of the maids who had to first payback her airfare to Singapore before she could start earning enough to send a pittance back home to her relatives.

I had told Lillian that I needed a place to work from on a part time come and go basis due to Steve's illness. If Steve was ill I would not come into the shop. She was quite happy as she said it was my self-employment and my time to do as I pleased.

It was becoming difficult for me to renew my visa in Singapore and so Lillian and I decided to open a business as I would then be eligible for a work permit visa. I was doing counseling and she was doing entertainment, so we made it a counseling and entertainment business. I did counselling and occasional helped out with dance classes but also did the bookings and helped arrange an International Belly Dancing exhibition.

Lillian often got money from dancing at functions and I was doing the same by doing entertainment at Functions. Singaporeans love to have a party and they usually hire entertainment, tarot readers, magicians and dancers to enhance the evening. My first event was an evening at the Singapore Women's awards. They requested that I dress to look like a gypsy. I was booked to be the entertainer for three hours. I attended many events in this way. The red carpet premiere of film "Pirates of the Caribbean" that I attended with a colleague, was one of the most memorable. Wearing our gypsy costumes we walked into the venue on the red carpet. The waiting crowds cheering as they thought we were actresses from the film, little did they know we were just the hired entertainment.

Steve:

I was travelling on business most weeks – despite the doctor's advice that I should not be. Whenever I got home from these trips I would have a meltdown. I used all my will power to hold it together during the week and then spent weekends in bed recharging. I felt desperately sorry for Bev. Here she had joined me in Singapore and I was basically a basket-case during the only times we could be together. I knew Bev was really enjoying Singapore as she would sit on the bed beside me at night and tell me all about her day's adventures.

Bev always says I am good at reading people the first time I meet them, and I did not take to Lilian at all. However, whatever reservations I had about Lillian's motives I was amazed at how quickly Bev was forging a life for herself. I was glad that Bev was active in her dance and that she was developing a life away from the tumour. It took a lot of pressure off me in that I did not have to worry too much about her getting bored sitting at the apartment all day – something that happens to a lot of expat partners when in foreign cities. Bev and I kept in constant touch with each other during the day with phone calls and sms'.

By getting out and about Bev didn't make me responsible for her happiness. She just got out there and got on with things.

CHAPTER FIVE
New symptoms

Find a place inside where there's joy and the joy will burn out the pain.

– Joseph Campbell.

Steve was due for his next radiation. He had been amazing at coping with his first treatment on his own. Steve could not remember much of what happened in the first treatment but he felt quite confident that as he had done it all before, he would cope easily with the second treatment. I did not have the heart to tell him that often the second treatment is worse than the first. The first treatment had taken its toll on Steve's health and his immune system was low. Although his eyesight and squint had improved tremendously, he was still badly uncoordinated in his movements. He would often bump into objects and people as he over -compensated his movements. He would lift his foot about half a meter more than was necessary to climb a pavement or step, this often lead to him tripping. Walking in the shopping malls he would hold onto my hand tightly but this didn't stop him bumping into people on his blind side and sending them flying. I did many apologizes. He would hold onto my hand so tightly that we often "caught" people who did not make the effort to walk around us but came straight forward thinking we would let go hands to let them through. There was no ways we would unlink our hands.

Steve was constantly battling with new symptoms. The doctors could understand Steve's pains but had trouble diagnosing them or giving him the right kind of medication to help him. The tumour was situated in Brain Stem where all the 'wiring' occurs. This Brain Stem is the center of communication from brain to body and is likened to a circuit box where the wiring had gone wrong so it was sending out 'false" messages from brain to the body.

Basically it was "phantom pains". Although called phantom pain, Steve really felt the pain in a very physical way. It was compared to an amputee who had lost an arm but could still feel pain or an itch in the arm although it was no longer there. Steve would experience huge pain at different times in various parts of his body. The doctors could not help with these because the brain was sending out false reports that induced these pains. Another of the symptoms that came from the tumour was that the brain stem also controls the body temperature. It was sending "Hot! Hot Hot!" signals to Steve all the time. Steve would get so hot and so the air conditioners always had to be on a very cold temperature setting.

Brain Stem nerves

These nerves are the "electrical wiring" system in all people that carry messages from the brain to the rest of the body. A nerve is like an electrical cable wrapped in insulation. A ring of tissue forms a cover to protect the nerve, just like the insulation surrounding an electrical cable. Nerves serve as the "wires" of the body that carry information to and from the brain. Motor nerves carry messages from the brain to muscles to make the body move. Sensory nerves carry messages to the brain from different parts of the body to signal pain, pressure, and temperature.

Steve had to go on a business trip to Kuala Lumpur, Malaysia. I went with him as I was still on a visitor's visa so needed to leave Singapore in order to renew it for another thirty days. We travelled with one of Steve's work colleagues. The horrid RP would join them later in the evening. Normally Steve stayed in central town when travelling to KL, for some reason on this trip the company had booked a hotel on the outskirts of town. It was a family fun resort. Steve had not been feeling well and I was so glad I was there to "watch' over him. It proved to be so fortunate that I had accompanied him on this trip.

We were shown to our room. We both burst out laughing as it was a theme room. It was kitted out like a wild western movie. The bed was shaped and made to look exactly like a wild western wagon, complete with canopy. The sides of the bed were high. There was no way into the bed but to climb in from the bottom which was the opening into the wagon. The walls were full of pictures of wild looking Indians, grim looking cowboys, detachable whips and cowboy hats. The window shutters were made to look like the swing doors of way gone saloons. There was even a pole sticking out of the wall and on it was a horse saddle. We were both so exhausted that we just crawled into the bed from the bottom. It was the most uncomfortable bed I have ever slept in, the floor would have been more comfortable. Given that fact that I am slightly claustrophobic being in a tight confined wagon was not the most romantic moment. The canopy also closed off all air ventilation to the bed. At 11pm the RP arrived at the hotel and in his usual egotistical and brutish way called for a business meeting. Steve had to get up and go to a no nothingness meeting and listen to the RP's rants. Finally it was over and Steve crawled exhausted into to bed at 1am.

The next morning, Steve crawled out of the bottom of the bed and set out with his RP and colleague for a day's business meetings in KL. I had to check out of the hotel on my own. I was going to another hotel in central KL to meet with Lillian's daughter, Colette. She had a job as belly dancer there. Steve was going to join me later as we would make our way back to the airport from there. Given the fact that Steve and I had different surnames, it was an embarrassing moment walking out of the theme room and asking for a taxi to be called to take me to another hotel. Strange, thing is that on our return to Singapore I looked up the "theme rooms" on the hotel website, there were none. The colleague had been given an Arabian night's theme room. We had no idea where the RP slept.

I arrived at the hotel to be met by Colette. We had a fun day as she showed me her dance routine and around the hotel. She introduced me to a young French girl who was the resident jazz singer. We were about to go for lunch when Steve called and said he would be collecting me earlier than planned as he did not feel well. When he arrived at the hotel I was terrified to see just how bad he looked, his face was drained of colour and he was shaking very badly. His speech had slowed down and it was difficult to understand what he was saying. We went to the platform to await the arrival of the train to take us to the airport and Steve started to sweat. The perspiration just flowed, within minutes he was drenched. I was terrified he was going to collapse and I saw that he was using all his will power to hold himself together. The train arrived just in time as Steve slumped onto the seat.

Although only a forty five minute flight from Singapore, it felt like was one of the longest flights home. Another symptom of the tumour had manifest.

The symptoms were indicating that there was added pressure to the brain and there could be no putting off the second bout of radiation. I had met Steve's neurologist Dr

Nasty and I had not formed a very good opinion of him. In my mind he seemed too opinionated, plain to say he did not have a good bedside manner. He was always rushed and refused to discuss any issues. It was simply done the way he said it was because he was the specialist. He did not explain or counsel because of this Steve did not know the details of his previous treatments he was just told to present himself at the hospital and at that stage it was about all Steve could do.

The preparation began in earnest again for Steve's second treatment of radiation. The week before he was due to have treatment he had to have another special mask made. It was molded to his face shape to keep the radiation from his face. It was so hard to watch him as a straw was put up each nostril for him to breathe through while the fiber glass hardened to fit his face shape. He also had to have more brain scans done before the treatment so a lot of time was spent in preparation.

The consultant radiation oncologist who worked out the amount of radiation Steve was to receive, Dr HK was wonderful. He would put up the scans and show me where the tumours were and explain how they were growing and what to expect. I think the worse thing about the tumour was that no-one could give any certainties as to what the outcome could be. He did at that time fear the worst and he made me face the reality. I was gripped with fear but I knew I needed to be strong. My strength came from suppressing the fear and not allowing it to engulf me. I had lost so much in my life I was determined not to give up hope or give into fear. I would fight alongside Steve.

Fear and loss were the emotions that dominated my young life. The feeling of not being able to control events that occurred in my life slowly fragmented me. I learned to be what everyone wanted me to be, a daughter, a wife, a mother but I was never truly my own person until I found that one component that could put me all back together again, Steve.

I so feared that now that I had found Steve, I would lose him and it was a brain tumour I was fighting and up against.

Steve:

The radiologist at the cancer center explained that the scans had shown that the tumour was still growing and that I needed to start another bout of radiation immediately. I felt a huge sense of disappointment but I knew inside that there had been no reduction in their size due the symptoms I was still having. At least my eye was moving slowly back towards its normal position. We booked my next bout of treatment and I went back to the office.

It was at this point that the anger hit me. Why me? Why now? I had Bev in my life and we were just starting out on a new life together in Singapore. I knew that another bout of treatment was necessary but was hoping against hope that there had been some shrinkage and we could just get on with our life together. The second stage of grief. Anger.

The purpose of the trip to Kuala Lumpur was to present our submission for a worldwide service RFQ to a major oil and gas service company. I was the only one from our company who knew anything about the industry. The RP and the rest of the bunch were just there to feel important and get their frequent flyer miles. The temperature in the conference room was set at 24C – I had a look at the thermostat when we entered in the room. Literally a minute before I started presenting I started shaking and the sweat started pouring out of me. I played a lot of sport all of my life but I had never sweated like this before. My shirt was hanging wet on me and I was using a handkerchief to wipe my forehead to keep the sweat out of my eyes. Fortunately most of the presentation was PowerPoint slides, so no-one was too focused on looking at me.

After the presentation I took a taxi to meet Bev at the hotel where she was visiting her friend. I was still shaking and drenched in sweat. We walked across to catch the KLIA Express to the airport. I was using every amount of strength left in me just to remain on my feet. I don't remember the train journey to the airport or the flight back to Singapore.

Chapter Six

Fear and loss

I was always looking outside myself for strength and confidence but it comes from within. It is there all the time.

— *Anna Freud.*

When I was five years old my world was about to be shattered my beloved father was leaving us. He was going away, I sobbed and sobbed. I was so young but remember the day he left vividly. I held his hand walking step by step with him until he had to leave. I clung to him and would not let go of him and had to be pulled away. I saw him walk away through a haze of tears. I refused to go inside but sat by the gate on my own. I cried until there were no tears left to cry. I often wonder if I had a premonition, maybe somewhere deep inside I knew that it would be the last time I saw my father.

When my father left home I had felt fear. I felt so alone and unwanted. Things happened so very quickly after he left, my mother remarried almost immediately. I was resentful and just felt that if "he" wasn't there my real father would be. I would not let myself love anyone I think it was the fear I felt of loss. My father leaving had depleted all my self-confidence and I truly believed that if my own father couldn't love me enough no-one ever would. My step father and I were in conflict from the beginning. I reminded him all the time of my father and he reminded me why my father was not there. It was a battle of strong wills. All photos of my father David disappear, I was told that my father had left us and I was never to talk about him again. I found out years later how broken hearted David had been by the loss of his little family.

A few months after their marriage my mother gave birth to a boy, Gary Vaughan. That baby melted my heart and I loved him. When Gary was six months old he developed gastric enteritis, he was very ill. My sister and I were left with relatives at home while my mother and step father took Gary to the hospital. They arrived home without Gary; my mother was hysterical with grief. She was holding a small package with Gary's clothes in it. He had died. It was hard to see my mother totally distraught, adults coming and going and hushed whispers. My sister crying so much but I was numb with that feeling of not belonging. I always felt like I was standing on the outside looking in. I tried hard to be the responsible one and take care of my mother and sister. I stayed calm, holding my feelings in and only crying when I was alone, silently into my pillow at night. I would take Gary's clothing out of the cupboard and fall asleep cuddled up with them, still smelling his sweet baby smell and longing for him. The fear engulfed me; I had loved and lost again.

A great grey cloud descended upon our household. At that point my mother just gave up. She could not cope and slipped into deep depression. She had lost her baby and the father she adored had died. He was only forty six and had a heart attack, she was in deep mourning. She lost all strength to cope and slept most of the time. She no longer sang, danced or read to us. During this period she had two more children in quick succession, a boy and girl.

I suffered another loss. My grandmother, whom I adored and was the base of my fragile security, met a man. They got married and went to live in Uganda to run a hotel there. Before she left, I went on a holiday with her to South Africa; a photo of me during that time shows me looking lost and bewildered. My Gran had met Uncle Geoff, an Englishman and he was twenty five years younger than her. It created quite a scandal as it was way before it was fashionable or popular to have a "toy boy". At the age of forty eight, she had invested in a new life for herself, a new husband, a new country. She lived a very exciting and adventurous life in Uganda. I did not see much of her once she moved but many years later, we moved to South Africa and lived in the same town and our bond was reunited.

We moved from Livingstone to Bulawayo Zimbabwe. Steve and I were moving in the same direction again; having been born just a few miles apart, we now both were moved to Zimbabwe. We lived in cities 443 kilometers apart, me in Bulawayo and Steve in Salisbury.

The situation did not ease between me and my step- father. He was authoritative and tried to force his religious belief system onto me. He had joined a religious group that distanced themselves from the rest of the "worldly people". There was always tension between him and me. We were both resentful of each other and now it was compound by the fact that I questioned his authority. I questioned things he told me and refused to accept what I did not understand. I still had the spirit and confidence to stand up for my own belief system as young as I was.

I went through years of trauma and tension but I never broke. I remained true to myself and my own inner core belief system and also hope. The thing that kept me going despite all the odds I faced was the fact that one day I would be old enough to find my father. In my worst moments I would dream of finding him and think about the love and protection he would give me. I created my whole world around that hope.

When, I was fifteen years old, I told my mother that I was so glad that I only had one year left of school as I was going to find my father. She replied without emotion, that my father had died one month after my fourteenth birthday. At the age of thirty six my father had suffered a massive heart attack and died. A part of me died then too, all hope had been extinguished in that one moment. I felt isolated, alone in having to deal with the greatest pain I have ever had to experience on my own. I was not allowed to mourn or be upset. Rather, I was told I was selfish and ungrateful and told that in reality my step father had always been a father to me not David. It just made me feel more resentful. I cried and cried and went into deep depression but it also gave me strength. It was an inner strength that allowed me to know and accept that I was on my own but I would survive. It was yet another parallel connection between Steve and I because at the same time, we were going through the same feelings of devastation, aloneness and confusion at the death of our fathers. Steve was eleven years old and I was fourteen when we both suffered the biggest loss of our lives.

Steve:

It was whilst living in Cape Town that I noticed for the first time the arguments between my parents. There was lots of shouting and screaming from my mother, whilst my father would just speak back at her in his usual calm talking pitch, even when she was trying to hit and kick him. There was something about this period that was also rather strange. My father had been invited to join Round Table, which he did as he was advised it would be good for his career. Suddenly my parents had a new group of friends. Apart from my father's work colleagues and his dive buddy, I did not really care for some of these new people. Little did I know how big a role one of them was to play in my life.

Then suddenly my mother, sister and I were living in Johannesburg on 13th Street in Parkmore, Johannesburg. My father remained in Cape Town. No-one would tell me why. I started school in Standard four at St. Davids, Inanda. No-one would tell me what was going on, but one of the men from Round Table in Cape Town was suddenly spending a lot of time at our house.

My eleventh birthday was coming up and my father asked me what I would like. I told him I wanted a ten speed for my bike, so he duly posted me Ten Rand to get it done. He was trying to be in Johannesburg for my birthday, but the company was having a conference over that time in East London, and he would come up after that.

On the 25th February 1969 my mother, on a very rare occasion, let me stay at home to welcome my dad. I had not spent the ten Rand on a ten speed so I rode that morning up to Mr. Underwood's' Toy store. I spent four Rand ninety nine cents on a Kodak camera and film to take photos of my father. The ten speed could wait, I wanted to see my father.

As I turned into our road on my bike with Rusty running alongside me my heart froze. The road was lined with cars and the epicenter of all the activity was our house. I knew immediately that my father had passed away. I dropped my bike on the front lawn and ran inside demanding to know where my father was. My godfather, and my dad's best friend, Uncle Chick grabbed my shoulders and came down to my level and told me my father had died.

It was the worst moment of my life. I asked how and he replied in a car accident. My mother was screaming hysterically and burst out "Don't lie, he shot himself". My world was over. My super-hero was gone. I broke free and ran outside grabbing my bike and pedaled away with a bunch of businessmen trying to stop me.

I went and sat in the veld with Rusty and cried myself dry. I eventually rode slowly back home. My godfather hugged me and said that maybe it would be better if I stayed with his family for a few days. With my mother still hysterical and my young mind trying to put things into perspective and make some logic of what was going on I thought it best as well.

For some reason my mother would not allow me to attend the funeral. I was not allowed to mourn my father at all. Instead I was back at school two days later, where word had got out that my father had passed away. At first break the main junior school gang gave me a beating for being an orphan.

As I washed away the blood from my nose and eye I wondered just what was going on in my life. It was about to get a lot worse.

CHAPTER SEVEN

Second Radiation and becoming a common law wife.

Our greatest glory is in never falling but in rising every time we fall

– Confucius.

Steve's second round of radiation treatments started again in 2006. Our short honeymoon phase where we just enjoyed being together and pretending that life was normal and trying not to mention "the tumour" was over. We were forced to face reality and the fact that the tumour was growing and urgently needed another phase of radiation. So the treatments began again.

Each morning we would arrive hand in hand at the hospital. Steve dressed in his long sleeved shirt and tie ready to go straight back to work. He had arranged to have his radiation early morning so that he could be at work at the required time. Having worked as a Hospice caregiver and counselor, I really doubted Steve would be able to go to work straight after treatment. I had often had to take patients to hospitals for their treatment. They would come out of the radiation room and hurry to the washroom. They would spend a long time in there and you could hear the sound of their violent vomiting. I always carried plastic bags with me as often the patient would vomit in the car on the way home. I would get them home and into bed where they would often stay until the next treatment. Not Steve; he walked into the oncology department looking so fit and well. His beautiful blue eyes retaining their sparkle as he greeted the staff.

I would go into the radiation room with him. Steve would lay down on the hard bed and I stood next to him holding his hand. They first covered his face with the protection mask they had made especially for him. It was covered with a square Perspex box which they then screwed into the table. I then had to leave him. The heavy radiation room doors swung shut leaving Steve alone inside. I could not hold back the tears as I waited looking at the radiation lights go on and off. I just couldn't even begin to imagine what it must be like for him. I watched as another man finished his treatment in the next room and came out looking pale and ill and rushed straight for the washroom where he vomited. Eventually, Steve walked out readjusting his tie and gave me a big smile and a cheery "see you tomorrow!" to the staff. In the cab afterwards, I could see that he face was bright red and he was shaking but trying his best to control the effects.

So the second treatment continued, five days a week for the next four weeks. Each day Steve would go straight to work afterwards but just collapsing into bed when he got home in the evenings. Getting into bed did not help much because the radiation seemed to over stimulate the brain. It is a rare tumour and difficult to treat as it was creating havoc with its constantly changing symptoms. At this point the best way to describe how Steve was reacting to the tumour was to refer to the movie "Phenomena" starring John Travolta. Steve's brain was mentally overly stimulated; he was reading up to five books at a time. It was almost like speed reading and he was reading them with absolute understanding and clarity. The pain was always there, deep neurological nerve pain, body aches, the most disabling headaches. Pain! Emotional, spiritual, physical and mental pain! Yet, he never once complained. It was so hard for me to watch the man I love in such deep pain. I knew that ultimately he had to get through this on his own all I could do was give him all my love and support. At this stage, we held the firm belief that the radiation would destroy the tumour completely and life would return to normal.

Strange how there will always be the best and worst of human nature displayed in stressful circumstances. In dealing with Steve's tumour we experienced the very best as well as the very worst. As well as dealing with the radiation treatment we were experiencing problems in both our working lives. Steve's RP was becoming more demanding and less understanding of Steve's treatment. He never asked about it, his only concern being that Steve arrived on time to work each day. He was completely annoyed and irritated by the very few days that Steve just could not gather enough strength to get out of bed. One Sunday evening, he phoned Steve and ranted at him about business for over an hour. He ended the conversation by saying "Your illness is making me sick too!"

This was grossly unfair as Steve was still achieving well for the company. He was still travelling for them even though the radiologist had warned against this. It was not advisable for Steve to do air travel because of the tumour's position. It caused him to get less oxygen to the brain and as the oxygen levels are kept lower on a plane, there was a real fear of him collapsing on air flight due to lack of oxygen. Air travel would result in disabling headaches. It didn't help that very few people in the company knew that Steve had a brain tumour.

DR HK was in charge of accessing the amount of radiation Steve needed. The amount was very high, too high as we later found out. I would often talk to Dr HK while Steve was having his treatment and I mentioned that Steve had been in tremendous pain the night before. He told me with the amount of radiation Steve was receiving I should not be sleeping next to him. I could not tell him that we had done a lot more the previous night than just "sleep together".

He would have been horrified. As with most things Steve experienced the opposite, the treatment rather than deplete his sex drive only served to heightened it.

Unfortunately before Steve treatment was completed Dr HK was transferred to another country and he was replaced by a new radiologist. He had no "bed side manner" whatsoever and was mean and obnoxious. He often hurt Steve badly while fitting the mask before treatment and did not apologize. He would be talking and joking with his colleagues while he programmed the radiology on the computer. I was terrified he would make a mistake. After one treatment Steve asked if he could change his appointment the next day for an earlier time. The radiologist signaled signs around his head to indicate that Steve was "crazy" to other patients. We heard much later, that he had been treating other patients with disrespect and he was fired.

Working from Lillian's shop had been fun and gave me a focus outside of the tumour. I was free to come and go as I pleased. I started to get a large cliental base and was bringing in a lot of money for our joint entertainment company. Instead of receiving my earnings daily, Lillian decided that they would be put into a bank account and they would be divided fifty percent between her and I at the end of each month. It was only my earnings going into the account and none of her earnings from dance and entertainment. I was not in a position to argue with her as the company we had formed together was the reason I was allowed a pass to stay in Singapore. Lillian became more demanding about the times I worked and would often over book me. She then started to take rent money from the amount I earned before she divided the rest between the two of us.

I was going to work after Steve's radiations treatment. I would often need to go the doctors or hospital on the way home to collect Steve's medication and refill the oxygen tank he needed. Lillian demanded I work a full six day week. If I told her that I needed to collect medication for Steve she would give me exactly one hour to do so. She always threated that if I did not comply she would close our business and report me to the authorities as not having a work pass. That would mean I would have to leave the country and it would have been devastating. It was taking a toll on my health. I began to lose weight and looked painfully thin.

The final crunch came when Steve was ill in bed and I called in to say I would not be at work. Lillian was furious and shortly afterwards I received a phone call from her Turkish husband who told me to get to work immediately. When I refused he called me a "Lazy Bitch!" That was the final straw. I did not go back to the Arab street shop again. I dissolved the company with great difficult. I managed to open up my own company thanks to advice and help received from my wonderful book keeper.

This lead back to the original problem, the need to have my visa renewed every thirty days and this could not go on indefinitely. The only other way for me to remain in the country besides getting a full time job was to become a dependent of Steve's. We found our way around this by legally making me his common law wife. This was no small task; we just couldn't say we were common law couple it had to be done before a justice of peace. It really was a long and troublesome process. We went into the "heart land" area of Singapore and went up to a dodgy office overflowing with files and documents. It was a very serious affair and after making several oaths and declarations, we were duly announced as common law husband and wife. It was more stressful and detailed than our actual marriage service a year later. We went out for lunch afterwards chuckling at our new status. Growing up one of the very worst things to be called was "common" and here I found myself a "common law wife". At least, it insured that I stay on in Singapore as Steve's dependent.

Steve:

The second treatment started and I was back into the routine again. Early morning treatment, office, home, collapse into bed. In the evenings when I could make it I would crawl up the stairs to the rooftop deck and lie on my back in the Jacuzzi with my eyes closed. I had an affinity for water. I always sought the solace of a body of water or the sea when I needed time for reflection, or just even time out. I found so much comfort just lying there. The pain seemed to let up for that short while, but then I was reminded me of what the tumour was doing to my body when I got out and went downstairs.

My company could not get me a Dependents Pass for Bev as we were not married so we decided we would look into whatever legal avenue we could to get her a pass. We found out we could get this done by making Bev my common law wife. I don't think Bev liked the "common" bit, but at least she was now legal and could stay in the country without having to carry on doing the thirty day visa-run.

I really did not want Bev to work, but I saw how happy it made her, plus even though I was earning a good salary I was not on a medical aid. Our provider had deemed my condition to be "pre-existing" and refused me cover. This was when RPs true colours' came to the fore. He had told me that even if the medical aid company refused me cover he would sort it out. I called his office and asked his PA for an appointment to discuss it with him. She called back a minute later to tell me he was not interested in my problem and I should sort it out myself. Nice – especially when my fledgling vertical was already totally outperforming established verticals in terms of ROI and margins. So Bev's financial contribution was most welcome.

By now I had cashed in a couple of insurance policies to pay all of the many scans I had to undergo on a regular basis, as well as the radiation treatments, as the hospitals demanded payment up front or no treatment. This was where I had to thank Singapore's wonderful banking system and their willingness to hand out credit cards. One Saturday morning Bev and I were in a shopping center and Bev went into one of the shops. I was waiting outside watching the world go by, wondering how I was going to be able to continue paying all of my mounting medical bills, as well as my monthly payments for family support back home. I had asked if I could catch up on payments for family support once I had found employment again but the reply I got was "don't use your tumour to try and make me feel sorry for you!" so that was not an option. I needed money urgently. I noticed two young men at small table with banners advertising one of Singapore's top banks. The passing trade got a bit quiet and one of these young men approached me and asked if I was a tourist or working in Singapore. I told him I was on an Employment Pass. He asked if I had a credit card from his bank to which I replied in the negative. He asked if I would like one and I told him yes. He asked if he could make a copy of my employment pass. I handed it over and went off to make a copy.

He came back and handed me my Employment Pass, asked me what my salary was, filled in my home address on a form, and asked me to sign it. I did this and he thanked me and informed me my card would arrive within ten working days, which it did, with a rather large credit limit. So with a few additional cards I would control the large financial outlays I had to pay for scans and treatments without stressing so much every time I had to surrender a policy.

CHAPTER EIGHT
Supportive friends

"Sometimes the questions are complicated and the answers are simple."

– <u>Dr. Seuss</u>

Steve was very ill and still battling with his working environment. The future was uncertain and I really felt I needed to be able to continue working even if just part time. When I was working for Hospice one of the most important things we needed to establish with our patients was their support systems, this was for both the patient and the care giver. A care giver needs support in order to be able to cope with all the physical and emotional aspects of taking care of a critically ill person. I was alone in a strange country and beside the doctors and nurses I had no support system. My three sons wrote me long fun filled emails about the happenings in their lives, they also sent me lots of encouragement but they had never met Steve. I did not fill them in on all the details of what was happening. They were worried enough about me leaving all to live in a strange country with a man they had never met who had a brain tumour. I kept my letters to them light and full of fun about my daily life in Singapore. I looked so forward to receiving their mails and hearing about the "normality" of their lives, most of all the shared laughter and the love they had for me kept me going.

I was alone in making huge decisions concerning Steve's treatment. It was scary and emotionally draining for me. I just needed someone, somewhere to give me a bit of emotional support and encouragement. Steve had a cousin Linda, who was living in Singapore. Steve had never really got to know Linda as she was the daughter of his late father's sister so they had grown up apart. It was so sad that they too had to meet under the trying circumstances of Steve's tumour. We met up on a few occasions but mostly Steve was too ill to socialize.

I met Linda and her husband John soon after my arrival in Singapore. Steve took me to meet them at an Indian Restaurant called Sammy's. Sammy's was a very basic restaurant that was set up in what used to be old Colonial army offices club. As usual it was a hot barmy night and we sat at a table outside hoping for a bit of breeze. I was taken aback when they served the food, a banana leaf was placed before each of us and then the waiters came out with a succession of huge pots which they ladled a spoon full of food from each pot onto the banana leaf. It was delicious though. The food was good, the company was good and I was drawn to Linda's serenity and calmness.

On another occasion we had been out to supper with Linda and John, the restaurant was in a vibie center of Club Street,

China Town. We were horrified to see how brightly lit the restaurant was, it was like sitting under bright sunlight. That is another custom that is often seen in Singapore. The restaurants must be brightly lit, so you can see the food you are eating. If it is not then they are suspicious that maybe the food is not so good and that you are trying to hide something. It's consider a good restaurant if you are to be able to see what you eat. The rule is the brighter the better.

We had a wonderful evening of eating, chatting and drinking a few bottles of wine. We walked out of the brightly lit restaurant into the dark evening night. We were readjusting our eyesight when Steve suddenly exclaimed that there were two taxis waiting. He told John and Linda to take the first and that we would take the second. With a wave of his hand, he went on his way while we all watched fascinated. The first car waiting was a taxi but as Steve found out very quickly to his surprise as well as the driver of the other car, was that he had in fact climbed into the back of a police vehicle. The night ended with hysterical laughter.

Linda became a good friend to me and she was a great emotional support. She would meet me for lunch and encourage me. I was so very grateful to her and always will be for her ability to calmly reassure me. Unfortunately, just as I really got to know and rely on her support, they left Singapore to retire in New Zealand. She became "IT". I had jokingly told her that as there was no-one else I could vent to, she would have to be it. Linda is the person I can email and who remains supportive and encouraging. Linda is kind, gentle, accepting and nonjudgmental. She is always there for me to express my fears, my sadness, my confusions and share in my joy.

I had met Neena at Lilian's dance studio. She was an elegant Chinese lady, who had taken up belly dancing as a hobby to keep fit. She was a TV commercial "actress". She had seen the bad way I was treated at Lilian's. This gave her the determined to help me and introduce me to life in Singapore. Steve's situation and health were a cause for concern. There was a lot of uncertainty about the tumour as after radiation the symptoms got a lot worse rather than better. Steve was exhausted by having to hold it all together and began to spend more time in bed. He needed the bed rest over the weekends in order to be able to cope with the work week ahead. I needed to continue to have clients because there might be a time when Steve could no longer work. I knew that isolation would not be good for me besides I enjoyed being able to advise others and give them some hope. Contact with other people benefitted me too as it helped me to focus outside of the tumour. Neena encouraged me to continue with my counselling however I no longer had a "place" to work from.

The greatest thing about my local Singaporean friends is that they talk straight. There is no need for them to embellish or refrain from saying things for the sake of politeness. They tell you the truth. They simply say it as it is. Other cultures may find this offensive yet it is never meant to be so. It's the way it is.

The Asian dress sizes are super small. In European sizing I take a size medium but when it comes to Asian sizes it's an extra-large. The first time I went shopping for a dress in Singapore, I saw a dress I wanted to try on. I asked the shop assistant, "Excuse me do you have this in a larger size!"

She looked me up and down and replied; "No, it's you who are big and fat!"

That simply meant; don't blame the size of the dress. It wasn't meant as an offensive statement rather a matter of fact.

In Asia, one is often told, "wow, you are fat!" or "you have put on weight". It is not offensive but a complement as it means that you have enough money or wealth to buy food to eat. In fact saying that one is skinny or has lost weight is an insult as that means they cannot afford to feed themselves.

Neena took me under her wing. She shook her head and said that I had been so busy taking care of everyone else I had forgotten to take care of myself. She told me that I needed to visit her doctor because my face was falling off. She took me to see her doctor Doc. Doc was a TCM doctor (Traditional Chinese Medicine practitioner.) Neena introduced me and explained the sad circumstances of Steve's tumour. Immediately Doc called me "Poor Thing" and he called me that on all my future visits. Later when he was explaining the various methods of TCM to me and questioning me each week on what I had learnt from him, he would call me "Doc". From then on depending on his mood I was called either "poor thing" or "Doc".

On the first introduction Neena explained her concern that my face was "falling of", meaning in need of nourishment. So Doc decided that the best thing for my face would be acupuncture. Doc inserted about twenty needles into my face. I reckoned that for that amount of needle's to be inserted my face must surely be "falling off" in a big way. I lay with my eyes shut I couldn't have opened them anyway as there were needles everywhere. He attached the needles to a machine that sent electro impulses into them. My facial muscles were jumping all over the place. My upper lip was doing a serious Elvis wobble impersonation all on its own. After many weeks of these treatments the Doc was very happy with the improvements to my face. He announced with pleasure that it was even getting rid of my freckles. He was most amused at my reply. "Oh no please don't get rid of my little bits of Africa!"

The TCM clinic with the gentle Doc and nurses became my once a week place of healing and refuge. There was a smell of herbs and spices all infused into a variety of medicines to cope with all sorts of problems. Each week I would have a different type of therapy, depending on what the Doc thought would be best for me. I was often put onto a huge therapeutic bed which had a fusion of medicinal herbs boiling underneath it. It would enfold me in a haze of steam and heady smells. This has always been a

Chinese remedy for body aches and pains. In ancient times, the Empress would sleep on this type of herbal bed every night. A young maid would be employed to make sure that the steam continued throughout the night as the Empress slept. I really don't know how she managed to sleep as the steam was extremely hot and lead to a very heavy sweat, I could barely last the required hour. During my treatments I thought of the expression; "what doesn't kill; cures!"

Another time I had burning charcoal sticks smudged along my face, arms and legs. The nurses were so gentle and compassionate. Once I was so exhausted that I fell asleep during a massage, the nurse did not wake me. She covered me with a blanket and left me to sleep. I woke up at 6.30pm and she was patiently waiting for me.

The most frustrating thing about Steve's illness was the very well meaning "advice" Steve received from others. He would be told about some new amazing herbal or medicinal medications or vitamins that would cure his tumour. Believe me, he tried it all. The thing about these "miracle cures" was that they were always so overpriced and expensive. There were never any improvements with any of the products we tried and in fact more often than not they only made Steve's symptoms worse.

Still we pursued any avenue we were told about. Christian prayer groups, mediation, acupuncture, massage, Hindu statues given to us for healing, soothsayers, ampules and everything weird, wonderful or just totally bizarre. I even persuaded Steve to go for ancient American Indian chanting Healing session which didn't help him at all as he spent the whole session trying to contain his laughter.

We went to a Chinese Herbal shop in pursuit of a cure. These herbal shops contain all sorts. Huge bottles of dried scorpion, dried snakes, a whole variety of dried mushrooms, dried sea horses, dried fish, dried shark fin and birds' nests. Medicine was made by the herbalist doing a rough kind of "diagnose" which is made by mainly looking at the palms of the hand and eyes of the "patient". Once this has been made it's a handful of this and a handful of that from the many bottles, which is then ground into a paste. The herbalist decided that as well as his selection out of his many bottles, Steve also needed an urgent neck and back massage. He put Steve onto a chair into the center of his narrow shop and proceeded to knuckle massage him. I could see Steve was in agony but before I could say anything, Steve was up and out of the chair. He said to the herbalist…"OK, you have hurt me enough! NOW it's your turn to sit in the chair while I massage you!"

A shocked herbalist looked on as I quickly took Steve's hand and we departed the shop!

Steve was still traveling for his company and his health suffered a huge set back after he had a business trip to India. He had to travel to many of the cities. He had heard all about "Deli Belly" and so was very careful about what he ate, avoiding the water, even the ice cubes. The night before he left he decided to get a take out from a western outlet. He got serious gastric enteritis from it that lasted for months. No antibiotic seemed to be abe to completely destroy the bug.

Steve and I had also traveled to Bangkok together, we carefully avoided "street foods" and had supper at the hotel the night before we left. We spent the night in agony, having to take turns throwing up in the bathroom. We arrived totally spent and ill at the airport awaiting our flight home. Besides these gastral pitfalls of travel, Steve was building up an intolerance to certain foods and spices.

I took Steve to my TCM Doc, he tried out many treatments on Steve. One involved electric shocks to the soles of his feet. The massage sessions left him unable to move for days afterwards. Everyone loved Steve though and looked so forward to his visits to the clinic. They loved the way he made them laugh and the fun he brought into the clinic. He left a legacy at the clinic in that he invented a name for some disgusting TCM medicine the doctor had given him to restore his immune system. It was really vile tasting but Steve persevered for a while. The doctor asked him about how the medicine was helping him and Steve replied that it was "bloody awful!"

The doctor laughed so much at that. I never knew the name of the medication but from that day forward it became known as "Bloody awful". Even when Steve was not there I heard him asking the nurses to mix some "bloody awful" for other patients.

The directions of how to use the Chinese herbal medications were lost in translation and were hilarious to read.

One of Dr Doc's nurses, Chu-Hua tried to talk to me. She managed to get across that she needed a counselling session from me. It proved impossible as she could not talk English and I could not speak Chinese. Neena said she would act as translator but where to meet? Chu-Hua came up with the idea that we could meet at her parent in-law HDB (Housing and Development Board) estate garden area. On the arranged day, I jumped on a bus to meet Neena at her bus stop. Neena had taught me how to use public transport. I was now comfortable enough to allow myself to settle into my seat on the air conditioned bus and watch the BBC tv program that was showing. Neena was waiting for me at her bus stop and we continue the journey together as we hopped on and off three other busses to get to our destination.

The majority of residential housing developments in Singapore are publicly governed and developed managed by the Housing and Development Board (HDB). About 85% of Singaporeans live in these estates. These flats are located in housing estates, which are self-contained satellite towns with schools, supermarkets, clinics, hawker centers, and sports and recreational facilities.

Public housing in Singapore is generally not considered as a sign of poverty or lower standards of living, as compared to public housing in other countries. Property prices for the smallest public housing can often be higher than privately owned property in other developed countries after currency conversion.

Chu-Hua was very welcoming and presented us with a welcoming rose water drink. It was very sweet sticky, kind of milkshake looking stuff. After the bumpy bus rides all I managed to do was sip it slowly. Once all the welcoming formalities were over, we got down to the talking.

We found a very quiet area on the edge of the estate. I started to talk to Chu-Hua with Neena doing the translation, a very slow progression. I really tried to concentrate on the whole process. Neena started to make very annoyed clicking sounds and shaking her head. I was beginning to wonder what I had said or done to offend. I asked her; "is there a problem?"

She replied "this just isn't going to work. You really do not look like one of us, you stand out! Now, look at the crowd you have drawn!"

I looked around me and old people from all over the estate had gathered around us. Some were sitting on the lawn close by, others on benches near us and all just staring at me. Neena said we had better move before someone reported that we are holding a public gathering without official permission.

In Singapore, one has to have police permission to hold a public function. You cannot just dance in the street as that will be classed as a public performance. You will receive a hefty fine for breaking laws. Singapore does have a speaker's corner, unlike the one is Hyde Park London where anything goes, rules are in force. I have yet to witness anyone talking from speaker corner in Singapore.

Public Speaking rules in Singapore

In order to have any form of public speaking such as a lecture, talk, address, debate, discussion, a play-reading, recital, performance or exhibition at Speakers' Corner, Hong Lim Park the following rules need to be complied with:

(a) The speaker must be a citizen of Singapore;

(b) The speaker does not deal with any matter —

(i) Which relates, directly or indirectly, to any religious belief or to religion generally.

(ii) Which may cause feelings of enmity, hatred, ill-will or hostility between different racial or religious groups in Singapore;

(c) **The speaker speaks using only any of the 4 official languages in Singapore, or any related dialect; and**

(d) **The speaker does not display or exhibit, or cause to be displayed or exhibited (whether before, during or after the public speaking), any banner, flag, poster, placard, photograph, film, sign, writing or other visible representation or paraphernalia which contains any violent, lewd or obscene material.**

Neena called a friend of hers, Bao. When Bao heard about what happened she told Neena that we must go at once to her HDB apartment. She said I could continue the counseling session there and invited us to have some lunch with her afterwards. So Neena, Chu-Hua and I jumped on yet another bus going in the direction of Bao's apartment. I was made to feel very welcome. I was still "new" to Singlish (Singapore/ English slang) and customs and sayings. I was puzzled by Bao's welcome... "Hello, have you had lunch Lah?"

My mind was probing for the right kind of response, I mean she had just invited us for lunch hadn't she? All I could manage was "pleased to meet you!"

The years have proved how pleased I was to meet wonderful gentle nurturing sweet smiling Bao, a true treasure!

Neena and Bao both translated all I needed to tell Chu-Hua as well as throw in some of their own valuable advice. Bao then said we needed to have lunch. Bao first apologized for "the simple meal" It certainly was not simple, she served a feast. It was divine and I have yet to taste any better fried rice than Bao's, she makes the best. My mind exploded with "yummie! Yummie! at each mouthful I ate.

Three of the main Singlish words used are CANNOT, DOUBLE CONFIRM and LAH.

Cannot is usually said first to most requests and used in a word bartering way. An example of this would be the following conversation between two persons;

"Can you meet me at 2pm Lah?"
"Cannot Lah"
"Can Lah"
"Cannot Lah"
"Can Lah"
"Ok Can Lah!"

Lah is said behind each sentence. It is used as a sign of agreement, a question or exclamation at the end of a sentence.

"Double confirm" is said to emphasie what you are saying is important and correct. Even more so correct if you say "triple confirm"

The use of these three words in your conversation will get you high praise indeed for your knowledge of Singlish!

Neena and Bao met twenty years ago when they had taken up the same cooking classes and they remained firm friend since. That first luncheon was the beginning of many. They chatted away in Chinese, throwing out a few English words for me to follow or stopping completely to translate. Bao commented that she was sure she had meet me once before when she came into the Arab street shop but I had looked older and not as radiant as I looked now. Neena looked very pleased and asked me if she and Chu Hua could share my "secret". I agreed so she told Bao that was because I was going to "the doctor" for acupuncture to my face once a week and that is how we met Chu Hua. They all discussed me and agreed there had been a great improvement to my looks. Neena added the dramatic effects by saying "Yes, you should have seen her before she looked just like a panda bear with those dark circles around her eyes!" So began my regular Thursday mornings with my new found friends. I so looked forward to them.

Steve:

Bev was really enjoying her adventures in Singapore. She was experiencing things from a different perspective that many expatriates do as she was making so many local friends who were introducing her to the "real" Singapore. I was really happy for her when she would excitedly tell me of the day's adventures when I returned from work in the evenings. It made Singapore come alive for me too as at this stage my life was just about work and trying to cope with the tumour's and medicinal side-effects.. We would laugh together at her daily experiences.

I could only imagine what things were like for her with me. Half of the time I was not fully aware of what was going on around me as I was so focused on trying to behave "normally" at work. There were less than half a dozen people at the office who knew about my tumour, and I wanted to keep it that way.

Bev would make my doctor's appointments, schedule scans, pick up my medications. She would argue with the various doctors we consulted who basically had no idea how to treat me, and force me to climb into a taxi with her to ensure I kept my appointments with my various doctors. I remember one of them looking at me and saying "you are over fifty, had good life, let it go". I was quite amazed by his simple philosophy. Here he was labelling me as old at fifty, as they do in Singapore. He would rather I went away and let whatever was going to happen to me and my tumour happen so he could concentrate his energies on treating younger people.

Bev had taken charge of the situation but she was making major decisions on my behalf on her own. She wrote long detailed emails to my family detailing my tumour, treatments and what was going on. They just did not want to hear about it. Out of sight and out of mind. The continued silence was deafening and I could see how much it hurt Bev.

It hurt me too and it was one of the many factors that led to a breakdown in relations with my mother and sister.

It was great meeting up with Cousin Linda and her husband John. I had only faint memories of Linda as she was a few years older than me and we grew up worlds apart. Linda reminded me so much of her mother - my father's beloved sister who had raised him – Aunty Joan. Both of them were just so calm and serene despite all of the losses they had experienced in their immediate family. Linda and Bev hit if off straight away, and Linda became a pillar of support for Bev in making decisions that would affect me.

Linda gave Bev great support and they became good friends. It was a sad day when Linda's husband John was transferred to Tokyo and Linda was no longer in Singapore for both of us.

In fact by this time Bev had gathered around her an amazing group of friends from different ethnic groups, religions, ages, genders and social levels. They were all special to Bev in their own ways.

CHAPTER NINE

Vasovagal collapses

You never read about real pain. It lives where no word can travel.

– Vanna Bonta.

Steve's symptoms were ever changing and growing worse as he was now experiencing vasovagal collapse. This was due to the restrictions and pressure that the tumour growth was causing to the brain. He could not sleep at all; he would go for five nights without any sleep. We tried everything to just get him to sleep but nothing worked. He would lie in a darkened room eyes wide open. His brain was so stimulated that sleep would not come. His headaches were acute and the nerve pain totally disabling. Every inch of his body was in agony and he was extremely sensitive to both light and touch. His immune system broke down and he was continually ill with flu or colds. There was only one word to describe Steve PAIN.

One evening, I was busy cooking supper and Steve was standing behind me talking. I sensed a slur in his speech and turned around in time to see him pass out. It was so weird one moment he was standing there and the next it was a meltdown as his body folded like a defrosting snow man to the ground. I could not move him, he was totally limp. I managed to drag him from the kitchen floor into the lounge area and sat with him until he came around. He had no idea what had happened to him. So began a new symptom, vasovagal collapses.

The brain was doing its own thing again. It was a temporary failure of the brain to maintain blood pressure and heart rate that caused the Steve to lose consciousness and fall. During these collapses the decrease of the blood pressure suddenly turns into a severe hypotension that is joined by a drop in heart rate that further worsens the situation. Brain circulation is impeded. Once he dropped to the floor, after a few minutes the circulation gradually restored itself to normal. Afterwards he would experience the after effects; often bleeding, feeling uncoordinated, extreme pain and anxiety and he would experience an unpleasant taste and smell that he could only describe as metallic.

The dangers of these collapses were that I had to make sure his airflow was unrestricted first. Then watch his breathing as there was a chance of him slipping deeper into a coma like state. I had to try and get him was sitting up and breathing properly in a short space of time. A bigger problem was protecting Steve from the physical injuries of his falls this proved almost impossible and there were many times he came down crashing onto his head. His body was always bruised by the impact of his falls and I had to deal with the bloody after mass of injuries. It was difficult as there was never a certain time or situation that triggered these attacks so they always came when we were not prepared. Steve is tall and so we came to learn that the taller you are the harder you fall.

The apartment we were living in had four floors to it. It was three flights of stairs to maneuver Steve's body up to the bedroom. The collapses happened with more frequency. One evening Steve went upstairs to shower. He did not return as soon as expected so I went to look for him and found him collapsed in a bloody heap in the shower. He hit his head against the shower wall as he fell; there was blood everywhere as head injuries tend to bleed a lot. He was lying face down in inches of water. It took all my strength to pull him out of the shower. I dried him as he lay on the floor. He had no strength or coordination to move, his body was a tangled limp heap. I pulled the sheet off the bed and turned Steve onto it. I gathered it together like a sling over his body and pulled the sheet slowly and with difficulty across the floor. Steve's motionless body was slumped and leaving a trail of blood across the floor as I pulled. When I got to the bed, I got onto the bed and pulled the sheet containing Steve bit by bit onto the bed. We both lay completely exhausted and drained.

A few weeks later it happened again in the shower. This time I did not have the energy, I could only pull Steve from the shower and dry him on the floor. I bought the duvet and pillows from the bed and made us comfortable on the floor where we both fell asleep exhausted. We were both always covered in bruises, me from trying to stabilize and move Steve and Steve from all the falls. The falls were now a major problem. They were happening more and more often. One evening, Steve collapsed in the lounge, that awful melt down. I managed to get him up and we walked up the stairs together bit by bit, stopping to rest every few steps. It took an age but at last Steve was tucked into bed.

I had an awful feeling that something was not quite right. He seemed to be in an altered state, not quite functioning. Early in the morning, he had a vasovagal collapse while lying in bed. I tried but I just couldn't get him alert. He was unconscious. In a panic I called the doctor, who told me to get him to hospital immediately, not to even phone the ambulance but to call a taxi as it would be faster.

The taxi arrived within minutes. He was such a kind man when I explained to him what was happening. He came into the bedroom with me and together we half lifted and dragged Steve's limp body down the stairs and pushed him into the back seat of the taxi. He lay slumped against me, unaware of his surrounding, slipping into semi consciousness and then unconsciousness. He was disoriented. I have never had such fear grip my heart and I really believed that we were not going to make it to the hospital in time. I kept calling Steve and telling him over and over again that I loved him and he had to stay awake. The tears were just running down my face and I had to use every fiber to remain calm and not scream out. The taxi driver drove like a F1 driver and got us to the hospital in no time, he ran inside while I waited with Steve. The emergency staff rushed out and placed Steve on a stretcher and wheeled him into the hospital.

Steve lay on the hard narrow bed in the causality emergency room, shaking so badly but at the same time perspiration pouring down him. His body was cramped up in agony. The medics gave him an emergency shot of Voltaren to stabilize him. It did nothing and seemed to make the reaction worse. I keep asking where his doctor was as his office was in the same hospital and they had been paging him to the emergency room. Steve's body was cramping in pain so I ran across the hospital to Dr Nasty's office to see what was taking him so long. He was having lunch. I yelled at him in frustration and fear, my voice breaking through my tears. I told him that Steve was in emergency room awaiting his urgent attention. He just looked at me and said he would be down in a while. There was nothing more I could do.

Back in the emergency room Steve received two Pethidine injections and it did nothing to relieve the nerve pain. Eventually, Steve was moved into a bed in the ward of the hospital to be kept in for observation. Many hours later, with Steve made comfortable in bed and propped up by pillows, Dr Nasty walked in. In his typical unfriendly manner he asked Steve to look at his finger and follow it as he moved it to the left and right, then asked him to stick his tongue out and move it left and right. He pronounced Steve well but was sufficiently worried enough to keep him in hospital for two days.

Once out of hospital, Steve would spend most of his time in bed unable to move, the headaches so debilitating. We had a roof top garden with a Jacuzzi and this was heaven sent for Steve as he would come home from work and just immerse himself into the water. It was his way of winding down after a day of holding himself together and getting through his work with sheer will power. He never once moaned or complained. I learned to give him his time alone in the Jacuzzi to restore himself before he would come down and join me. I often, felt isolated and so alone in dealing with it all. Hearing Princess Dianna on say in her TV interview that she felt "there had always been three of them in her marriage" resonated with me, there was Steve, me and THE TUMOUR.

Dr HK had told me that it would not be easy to cope with and that Steve would have very bad days. The problem is that the cavity area the tumour grew in is very small and so exerting a lot of pressure. The erosion on the adjacent petrous bone caused tremendous pain and the tumor has been there for some time. There could not be pain relief until the tumour had disappeared or reduced in size so that it no longer exerted the pressure. Dr HK explained it and demonstrated the effect by telling me to press my palm with my thumb for a long time. The indentation that remained there after I had removed the pressure was similar to the effect the tumour had on the petrous bone and surrounding areas. He told me that it's like the worst continual tooth ache you will ever have. The headaches shifted to different areas on his head. Steve was again told that he needed to take cortisone order to reduce the swelling on the brain and so he tried but once more he had a terrible reaction to it. His body just could not tolerate it.

The Tumour was responsible for pain, it was crippling, emotional, physically and spiritually. He advised that the only way I could deal with the hard times was to separate Steve from the tumour. I needed to understand that the wonderful man I had fallen in love with would always be there but the pain and all the problems it brought with it would always be the TUMOUR. The tumour was controlling Steve but Steve could not control the tumour.

Steve:

Basically overnight I stopped sleeping. I would go three to five nights at a time without sleeping, just lying there staring at the ceiling in the darkness with my brain incredibly active. I was unable to "switch off" and sleep. In Singapore the prescribing and dispensing of medications is extremely strictly controlled and medical doctors are "graded" according to their area of specialization as to what they can prescribe. Back in South Africa a pharmacist has more authority to dispense medicines than a General Practitioner in Singapore. An example of this is we found that Neurofen sometimes helped with certain of my symptoms so Bev would go to the pharmacy to buy some. The pharmacist would take her Dependent's Pass, type her number into the computer, and come back and say "Cannot! You buy last Monday. Can only buy next Monday"! It was frustrating but we had to laugh about little things like that. It could also be a very good example of what many other countries could do to stem drug abuse.

I had to get the chief radiologist at the Cancer Center to prescribe sleeping pills. We started with some mild sedatives which did nothing for me. We then moved onto Stillnox. Again – nothing. After much experimentation I found that Dormicum and Xanax helped. I went through one really bad patch when I was taking up to 4 Dormicum tablets per night and was still not sleeping. It was crazy. Strangely enough for me it was bizarre as I had never had any issues with sleeping before. When I was in the military and diving my colleagues were always amazed at how I could sleep anywhere, any time, and in any position. It was also really difficult for Bev as she is a very light sleeper and as much as I could do to lie still so as not to disturb her, I knew she was not sleeping either.

On the nights when I could doze off the body spasms would start. I could feel the spasm building up in my body, and then "Bam" and I would literally jump an inch or two above the bed. Bev could feel them as well. Then I would roll over and try and to get to sleep again, only to experience another one if I was lucky enough to start dozing off.

I started imagining my dream island in my head to try and tire my brain out. This special island became my refuge and escape, not only from my sleepless nights, but also as an escape from the pain when it was at its worst. Bev was aware of my island and when she could see I was battling she would encourage me to "go visit your island".

It was at this time that my "brain-fades", as I call them, started. I would come around and notice blood on the pillow, or bruises and cuts on my face or body and have no recollection of it at all. I would have to ask Bev what had happened and she would explain. It happened occasionally when I travelled as well. I would wake up in my hotel room, aches and pains all over, and would go and look in the bathroom mirror to carry out a damage assessment on myself. I would then try and think up an excuse for the bruises or cuts on my head to tell my colleagues and clients.

The worst thing about the tumour is that internally I was in constant pain – severe headaches, body pains, and the shakes, but outwards I looked fine. It is incredibly frustrating living in such a state. People had no idea what I was going through every minute of every day. Even signing off on documents was difficult as I would be shaking so much every time I signed something it was a different signature. I had to stop accepting a cup of tea or coffee in meetings as I could not even get the cup up to my mouth without spilling half of the contents all over the table and myself.

The oil and gas industry is a very social one, but due to the tumour and it's side effects I had to stop accepting invitations for drinks or dinner as I knew I would be shaking so badly I would struggle to even get the fork up to my mouth, and could not bring a glass of wine to my lips without holding it with two hands, so eventually my colleagues just stopped asking me.

CHAPTER TEN
Thursdays in Singapore.

In the sweetness of friendship let there be laughter and sharing of pleasure. For in the dew of little things the heart finds its morning and is refreshed.
— Khalil Gibran

Beverly:

My Thursdays in Singapore took me into a whole new world. I would catch the number ten bus arriving at the huge interchange bus station. Bao would be waiting there for me, together we would jump on the number twenty bus and then it was only two bus stops from her home. Bao met me at the interchange because it was so huge and I had got lost there before trying to find connecting busses. The interchange was a hive of activity with people waiting for bus connections. It had a market place as well as a wet market selling freshly caught fish and meat and animal carcasses hanging from huge hooks. There was a diversity of sounds and smells from all the little market stalls and bargain shops and of course the eating stalls filled with people having "lunch". Arriving at Bao's home I would leave my shoes outside the door, as most people do before entering a home in Singapore.

Boa's husband was ill and so he lay on the couch while we all sat around the dining room table. He loved the company and listening to the chatter. He would smile and chuckle along. He enjoyed Thursdays just as much as I did.

Neena and Bao met at cooking classes and I am told how they met Pearl. They speak in fast Mandarin Chinese, loudly with arm's moving to display actions and exaggerated expressions. Neena would throw out a few English words to me in translation but I followed their conversation by their movement, expression and sense of drama. They speak bluntly, not to cause offense but just telling it the way it is.

They laugh and each threw in bits to add to the story as its being told. Pearl says that when Bao's husband was still a young good looking strapping young thing twenty years ago, great chuckles here from him; he used to love to sing and so he would go to Karaoke every Saturday night. Boa was not so keen on singing so she would stay at home. At Karaoke, he met a lady who also loved to sing and they became good friends. She was Pearl, and she would often ask Bao's husband to bring his wife with him so that she could meet her. One evening, her husband having persuaded her, Bao went with to the karaoke evening to meet Pearl. Bao first went to the ladies room and there she got chatting to a lady. The lady told her that she was there to meet her friend's wife, not knowing that Bao was the lady she was due to meet. When the husband introduced them, they laughed because they had already met and from that evening on they have always been best friends. They would retell this story to me each week with just as much joy and laughter as the first time around.

Then, they want to know how I met Bao, I tell them I met Neena at Belly dancing classes, this bring a huge round of laughter and through her I have been introduced to Bao.

The table was piled with food, fried rice, and assortment of meat dishes. It's a meal of such flavor and wonderful texture. Neena had brought the desert she made. It's so yummy and the conversation so good. I feel very privileged to be brought into their intimate circle.

It was so wonderful to be part of the close circle of friends. My Chinese luncheons are magical. They take me to another place, another world. I feel unconditionally loved and accepted. I so wish I could tape the conversations. I could write a whole book on "Lunch on Thursdays". They really made such an effort to include me in everything. Each week Bao will apologize as she sets down the lunch. "Just a simple meal" she says but it's anything but that. The table is always loaded with spicy, delicious food. Once everyone has been given huge servings, the chatting begins, with loads and loads of Chinese green tea served all the time, the tea cup is never left empty. No-one ever gossips, that is a big no-no but still the stories slip out. It's a grand production of conversation with many splattering's of oooohs and aahhhs, and fierce expressions with nods of approval or disapproval. Its serious stuff at times too and I battle not to laugh.

Pearl, who fancies herself as a bit of an opera singer, will suddenly burst into a high note or two. No reason just the joy of exercising her vocals. She wears heavy makeup and is a fairly large lady, she reminds me of Mimi from the Drew Carey show.

She tells me the scandalizing story of her husband. He left her to live with another woman, whose husband was crippled and still lived in the house with her. They tortured the other woman's poor crippled man by sharing the house with him. Pearl added indignantly that it was not even her husband's fault; this dreadful woman must have put some kind of a spell on him to entrap him. She no longer wants anything more to do with her husband, so currently she is going out to sing Karaoke each weekend in the hope of finding a new husband. After the story she promptly breaks into song in order to impress us with her talent. To give you an idea, Chinese opera can sound like nine cats being swung by their tails and screaming at different pitches.

Over the weeks many stories emerge as Pearl relates her experiences at weekly Karaoke in the hope of finding a new husband. One Thursday morning we are joined by an "aunty". Old Chinese ladies are always called Aunty as a sign of respect. Aunty brings her cousin, Jade with her. There is great excitement because Jade is from America. She lived with her aunt in Singapore until she found herself a man on an internet dating line. She lives very happily with him now in LA where her favourite pass time is gambling.

Pearl was very interested to learn about the success of these Chinese ladies meeting husbands on the internet as she thought it might be less effort than her current Karaoke husband search. So began a long discussion of the pro and cons of internet dating.

Bao's step daughter was on her third American husband having met them all through the internet. The first one was not such a good choice as they had corresponded for a while before he invited her to America to meet him. Once she arrived there she discovered he was a cripple and after being married for a few months decided it was not for her so she returned home.

Husband number two, also met on internet was a "lovely chap" and moved to Singapore to be with her. Unfortunately, he got lung cancer and passed away at the young age of forty seven. Photos were being passed around and ooohhs and aahhs were sounded while looking at them. We got to see all the wedding photos and the funeral photos and the funeral program. We were shown a photo of him lying dead in his coffin. We were each expected to comment on the dead photo as a kind of respect and blessing.

Some of the comments were;

"Such a presentable looking youngish American"
"Poor chap dead at forty seven"
"What a pity he never had children of his own"
"Now he has gone"

After what was deemed a suitable silence, it was onto husband number three. Also an internet caught American. He came to Singapore where they had two weddings. One Western where she is dressed in the traditional white wedding dress and the other a Chinese wedding where they are both dressed in traditional Chinese robes. Photos are once again passed out for us to look at and commented on;

"He looks ok"
"He looks a bit like Alex Baldwin!"
"Hansom fella"
"How fortunate".

He is currently serving in the USA army in Afghanistan but sends loads of money "home" to her. Aunty does not like this conversation at all. She says this modern approach is shameful and she reminisces about times gone by and the correctness of family arranged marriages. When we turn to discuss another subject, Pearl continues to look at the photos again and again. You can see she is thinking about the possibilities of the internet.

Those luncheons became a part of my world. The Chinese chatter around the table, the encouragement and support they gave me, it was like a weekly dose of regaining strength and grounding. Sometimes they would request that I bring along my dancing veils and we would put on music. Laugher would full the room as we swayed and moved along with the colorful scarves to the music. I grew to love the place and the people and was so grateful to the universe for the new space it has created for me. I felt so blessed to be cared for and nurtured by this gentle group of friends. I was getting out and about and seeing the real Singapore, meeting wonderful people and not just stuck slave like in the back end of a shop in Arab Street.

These wonderful people were so kind, giving and generous. They had so little themselves but gave me so much. One day I mentioned that Steve loved Chicken pies. When I arrived the next week, Bao had made a whole batch of chicken pies for me to take home to Steve.

One morning I was sitting on the bus after having spent the morning listening and trying to understand what was being said in Chinese. I was feeling confident enough to try out a few of the words I had picked up. There was an old Chinese lady sitting next to me, small wrinkled all over, a tooth missing, straw-like thinning grey hair. She was smiling at me and tapping my arm in a caring motion.

I decided to be friendly and opened the conversation with nǐ hǎo, meaning "how are you?" in Chinese. If you have ever asked someone how they are then wished you hadn't, this was one of those occasions. She joyfully jumped at the words I had put out and she spoke and spoke and spoke. She must have told me how every member of her family was in this life time and previous ones. She was speaking in Chinese with lots of gestures and laughs. I did not have a clue as to what she was saying but this didn't seem to worry her at all. It was quite an amazing conversation by the sounds of it. I was so relieved when my bus stop came into sight but we parted good friends with the whole bus waving me off. That was my full attempt at trying to talk Chinese. When we were children and could not understand something we would say; "it all sounds Chinese to me" now I could really understand the value of that saying.

Neena often spoke to me about traditional Chinese beliefs and their various customs and Gods. She was eager to show me and so she took me on an educational tour. She first took me to a shop selling status of different deities and explained what each one did. It was fascinating but some of the gods looked very fierce and scary. She then took me to a huge temple, there were many fortune tellers sitting outside the temple. They formed a huge variety, face readers, palm readers, card readers, ancestor readers, destiny path, numerology, astrology. They all spoke in Chinese no English. We went up to one of the many flowers sellers outside the temple and bought some flowers to offer in the temple after our prayer.

We had to walk through a crowd of people standing at the entrance to the temple. They were praying, lighting incense and bowing before entering the temple. There were many people sitting on a massive carpet and shaking a tubular box that held many numbered sticks. The noise as we entered was deafening. The people were totally silent but there was a huge chick, click, chick, click noise of the wooden sticks being shaken. Neena went and got a box for each of us from the monk and showed me what to do.

On my knees I held the tubular box with two hands slightly at an angle. While praying I needed to ask a question. Then repeat the question over and over as I had to shake the sticks until one fell out. This took a long time and my knees and hands began to ache, eventually after much shaking a stick dropped out onto the carpet. I was not allowed to pick it up yet. I had to then hold two red pods in my palms and shake them. Then throw them dice like onto the carpet. While throwing them I had to ask "is this stick the right answer to my question?"

If the pods fall upright the answer is yes and you may pick up your fallen stick but if they do not fall upright the answer is no and you have to begin all over again. Mercifully, mine had fallen upright. My answer was correct I could pick up my stick, which I then took to the monk. He gave me a small piece of paper with the answer that corresponded to the number of the stick I held.

I left the temple smiling, my question had been "will Steve's health be restored?"

The answer I received was "***The sun shines after the clouds have blown away. The future is bright.***"

Neena also decided that I was getting fat so she organized for her and I to attend water aerobics held at the local public swimming pool. We would arrive early on a Tuesday morning, join a group of middle aged Asian women and be greeted by our instructor. I was certain that she had been recruited by the army as she was very fierce and very serious in her training of us. We all had to jump into the swimming pool while she walked up and down on the edge of the pool, shouting instructions at us and blowing loudly on her whistle at any infringements of these instructions. We had to take turns to haul each other across the pool fast and with no stopping, while the other was hanging on for dear life. We had to skip with a sponge pool noodle in the water. I thought it impossible but completed the action twice then stopped. That resulted in a shrill whistle blow and I was given an extra ten to do for stopping. The Asian women all wore visor covers in the water to protect their face from the sun and they found it very strange that I did not as I loved the feel of the sun on my skin.

After this hair rising and fierce exercise, we would hurry to the showers. Afterwards, we would walk across the road to the local food court and have our "lunch" which was usually divine Chinese deep fried dumplings; so much for our exercise.

Singaporeans love to save a dollar or two and are always on a look out for a bargain. My fifty fifth birthday was heralded by much excitement from my local friends as I now became a "golden Citizen". This enabled me to have reduced fees and discounts on most things. I could pay the senior citizen bus fare and sit in the specially allocated seats for "old people". I was given my pharmacy discount card. Neena was especially happy that I could now go to the public swimming pool and only pay an entrance fee of fifty cents as opposed to the one dollar I had to pay before I became a "golden citizen". I also got a reduction on my water aerobics fees. Old age was bestowed on me before I was ready to embrace it.

A few years later when Steve turned fifty five, I so enjoyed giving him a "golden seniors" card; I don't need to repeat what he said!

CHAPTER ELEVEN

NO light at the end of the tunnel.

Hope is being able to see that there is light despite all of the darkness

- Desmond Tutu

Beverly:

The second treatment was over at last but it had wreaked havoc with Steve's body. His immune system was so low and he was always catching infections as he was still going into work daily as well as traveling to many different countries on business. Steve's philosophy was simply:" it had to be done!" and he did it.

All we could do was take one small step at a time dealing with the worst effects first. It was so hard to see Steve in so much pain. It was painful for him to move, he walked slowly and carefully, each step causing tremendous pain. He was in pain when he was awake, he was in pain when he was asleep; it was relentless. He had full body sweating that drenched him in seconds, his hands shook so that he could not hold a pen and he had constant numbness in his face and hands. Not once did Steve ever show any sign of weakness, he was so brave and so inspirational to others around him. It was a tough period because Steve had financial commitments to his family and his huge medical bills to pay so he continued to work. I just did not know where he had the strength to carry on. We were both feeling apprehensive and exhausted but the lowest point was still about to manifest.

Steve's health was at a critical point, when one evening we were sitting downstairs. Steve went into the bathroom, when he walked out he announced, "My cousin K has just died".

It was a firm statement and I tried to tell Steve not to be silly as it was just his fears. He was insistent though that he just knew. The following morning we got a call from his cousin to say that her brother, K had suffered a brain hemorrhage and passed away the night before.

That night Steve had a massive vasgovagal collapse in the shower. Once more I pulled his wet blood soaked body out of the shower and onto the floor. He could not move. Lying on the shower floor he shouted out with huge primal howls in frustration, anger and sorrow. I left him alone, sensing he needed that time to himself as it was the first time he had released any of his feelings. I sat on the floor outside the bathroom door with tears flowing down my face. In that moment I had the dreadful fear that the tumour was winning. When Steve had vented his frustration he lay exhausted and spent on the floor. I helped lift his limp body and we slowly moved to the bed together but Steve emerged from that bathroom with a stronger resolve.

Steve has always had an uncanny sixth sense. When I had first moved in with Steve, he went away on his first business trip leaving me at home. I lay alone in bed and looking at the bedroom curtains I thought that they should be in the study and the study curtains should be in the bedroom as it would suit the colour schemes so much better.

Having just recently arrived into Steve's home I did not consider making the change...well, not just yet. But the thought was there.

Steve arrived home and putting his case down shocked me by walking up to the curtains and saying "Ok, so what have you done to the curtains?"

We laughed as I explained my thoughts about the curtains and how he just "picked up" on the feelings I had about them. He did think it was a great idea too.

Steve often picked up things on a more serious note as he had with K and the whole weekend he had a feeling that "something was not right". When he went into work on Monday, with no prior warning the RP said they would not be renewing his contract and he was to leave with immediate effect. One of Steve's worst fears had manifested, he was now without a job and expanding medical bills to pay as well as his family commitments.

It was one of the worst times of our lives. We were in Singapore on work visas which once you lose your job you have to leave the country unless you can get other employment or a local sponsor. We needed to pay Steve's income tax before we could receive his full salary. We did not have the lump sum amount. We had exactly zero until we received his salary. We made our way to the income tax office to plead our case and ask if Steve could do smaller monthly instalment pay backs. After a long wait and being shuffled into a small cubicle, the very serious tax man asked us to excuse him while he checked out Steve's case with the supervisor. Steve and I sat there waiting in nervous silence until we both saw a notice on the wall of the cubicle at the same time; *"There is NO light at the end of the tunnel. Due to the expense of electricity all lights have been switched off."*

It was probably the intensity of the moment but Steve and I found that the funniest thing ever and started to laugh. The taxman reappeared and seemed to be a bit puzzled to find Steve and I laughing our heads off. But he had managed to solve the crisis and phoned Steve's now ex company and demanded they pay him in full immediately.

Steve after a treatment on his way to the office

Steve:

K's death hit me hard. Apart the fact that he had died from a brain hemorrhage K was just a wonderful person. When I was diagnosed with my tumour the doctor told me my type of tumour, whilst extremely rare, was termed "familial". Familial as opposed to hereditary is that its definition is "tending to occur in more members of a family than expected by chance alone". So it can jump a generation or so then strike without warning.

My first thought was for my children. I had to tell them this fact so they were aware of it and could be timeously checked. I then started thinking that maybe this tumour had something to do with my father's and his two cousins'

126

deaths. Did they perhaps also suffer from a glomus tumour and its associated symptoms to the extent that they either took their own lives or had "accidents"? Unfortunately no-one in the family could, or would, answer all of my questions regarding these events. In those days such deaths were accepted and no-one looked too deeply into them, nor, heaven forbid, state that "Uncle Joe had something wrong in his head".

I have an incredibly high pain threshold. I was born like that but I suppose it was also honed into me as a child. My mother remarried a man who had no experience of teenage boys as he had only had daughters in his previous marriage. He had a vicious temper and I very quickly became a physical outlet for his temper rages. It was not just the occasional slap but a full punch in the face and to hell with the consequences. From the first beating I could not wait to leave home but I never showed any emotion when this happened, which just infuriated him more, and led to more beatings

Anyway, I would always be told by doctors prior to an injection or procedure that "this is going to hurt", and I would always reply was "No it will not". They would proceed as gently as they could and would be amazed when not only did I not flinch when the needle went in, but I would actually watch the whole process.

I was enjoying my job from an interaction with my team and clients point of view, but not from the corporate "culture" side. If you did not kiss the RP's ass and indulge in lot of high-fiving and back-slapping you were out. I am a quiet kind of person and would rather sit in the background and let my team get the credit for our success than participate in these little rituals. The RP and his bunch of senior VPs embodied everything that could be wrong with a company. If you were not in their inner circle you were basically regarded as worthless, and during my two years with them I saw them destroy the careers of many good people. They were merciless and did not base their judgments' on rational thought and the effects it would have on people's lives, it was rather whether they liked you or not.

I signed on with them on an initial two year contract, which had now reached its end and so we were to hold a review to see if they would offer me a new contract. I knew in my heart that it was not going to happen, and quite frankly I did not want to continue working for them. The tumour affected me so badly I had not had a chance to get my CV out to market and explore alternatives. My division, which I had started from a zero base was totally outperforming the established verticals in terms of returns and margins, but I know the decision would not be based on logical thinking.

I walked into my office early and saw that T, the VP of Sales for the region was in his office early. I walked across to discuss a few things with him as my assessment discussion was scheduled for that afternoon. T is a big guy and saw me coming across and quickly stood up and hitched up his trousers and placed his hands on his hips in a bit of a menacing stance. I am not the smallest person in the world either, and after what I have been through in my life such posturing did not intimidate me in the least.

T was actually a nice guy and he had drawn the short straw in the inner circle to give me the news. There was no review, just a statement from T that it had been decided not to renew my contract and that I could leave immediately. I put my hand out to shake his and say goodbye. This took him totally off guard as he had been expecting me to plead my case and beg for my job. I turned, went back to my office and started packing. My PA noticed what I was doing and came in with another Vertical Director to see what was going on. I told them and they both went back to their desks with tears in their eyes. With my boxes packed I called a cab, loaded them in and went home, told Bev what had happened and climbed into bed.

Bev was her usual calm and caring self when I gave her the news about the job. In her usual way she told me something would come up, but I sensed her concern. I was exhausted and realized I needed to rest. I spent a few days in bed, then one morning decided this was enough, got my laptop out, updated my CV and started registering on oil and gas job sites. The industry was in a bit of a slump so I was not feeling overly optimistic about securing a position in the short term.

T fell out of favour about a year later and was let go as well.

CHAPTER TWELVE
Gaining survival skills.

Open your eyes and look within. Are you satisfied with the life you are living

– Bob Marley

Beverly:

Both Steve and I had been very independent when we were young. Life had thrown us some difficult circumstances and we learned survival skills from an early age. I think this helped us to cope in dealing with his illness.

My life as a child became steady worse. There always seems to be a point where I had to be the responsible adult in taking care of my siblings. When I was eleven years old my much younger brother drank from a glass that had been filled with bleach. He was thirsty so gulped it all down in one go before the taste hit him. He was screaming in agony, my mother phoned a family friend, who came around immediately. My mother could not cope with it and so I was the one who went with to the Hospital emergency room. While my mother friend drove, I held onto my brother. She was telling me to keep him awake and talking. I was terrified, my thoughts going back to the death of Gary. I was so scared but I kept calm talking to him, telling him I loved him and that we were going to the hospital and it would be ok. Once we arrived I was left sitting alone in the emergency room while he was rushed into theatre to have his stomach pumped. I had visions of arriving home with just his clothes as my parents had done with Gary. It seemed like forever. I just sat in silence and waited, I did not move from the chair. It was such a relief to see my little brother emerge worn out, pale looking but alive and crying for me.

When I was fourteen, my mother told us she was pregnant again. My siblings were ecstatic at the thought of a new brother or sister. I just felt humiliated and mortified. Parents did not talk to you about sex in those days. To be faced with the evidence of my parents sexual activity at that age was dreadful. As my mother's pregnancy advanced I did not go anywhere with her in case my school friends saw me. The closest thing we ever came to a sex education was that my mother and her close friend Pam decided to take their daughters to see movie called "Helga" it was very advanced for its day. It showed a woman's journey through pregnancy and child birth. We were horrified at all the gory details and decided we would never have sex and children, so it must have had the impact that our mothers had wanted.

In 1967 a West German health minister called Käte Strobel decided to promote sex education using a sex educational movie called Helga. It was ahead of its

time as it showed a very graphic childbirth scene. It was amazing that it passed the strict censorship rules of those times.

The day arrived that my mother went into labour. We all got into the car with her and went along to the hospital. No children were allowed in Maternity hospitals so we sat on the lawn outside. After what seemed like ages my step father emerged and he was very serious and withdrawn. He picked up my aunt on the way home as she would look after us while he returned to the hospital. I just knew that something was not right as they spoke in whispered tones and both looked extremely worried. He arrived home later that evening with the news that we had a baby sister called Kim and that she would be home with us in a few days. It was not to be as Kim was born with under developed lungs and only lived for forty eight hours. My mother was still in hospital, seriously ill when we had Kim's funeral. Tears flowed as the little white coffin was carried in. It was so hard to accept and I felt a terrible guilt and burden that I had been so resentful about this pregnancy. I wondered if I had been punished. My mother could not cope emotionally. It was around the death of Kim that she had received the news that my father had died of a heart attack. She withdrew into herself again.

I was fifteen years old recently finished school when I had another disagreement with my step- father. It was the first time I told him that he was not my father. I went to my room and took down a suitcase and threw some of my clothes into it and left the house. I had no idea where I was going. I caught a bus to the city Hall center and sat it the gardens until sunset. I then went to a phone booth and called a girl who had been to school with me. Her parents had bought a large old house at the opposite end of the town. It had in the past been used as St Claire's home for unmarried mothers but they turned it into a hippie community center.

I was given a warm and "groovy" welcome into their "psychedelic" world. I shared a room with my friend. All meals were taken in a communal dining room with the weird and wonderful live- ins. They became my protective "family". I felt warmth and protection from these gentle people whose philosophy was "make love not war."

Because I was so young they quickly formed a band of protection around me. I was "chaperoned" everywhere. They educated me on the different types of drugs available so I could not say I had taken something by mistake. They told me that they were watching me and I was never going to take drugs. Although sex and drugs was very much a part of their culture they made sure it was not part of mine. They would send me up to my bedroom while they all went outside to smoke a joint. I was on the top floor and I would gaze out the window longingly. Wishing I could join them lying in a circle on the lawn gazing up at the starry night sky while they passed around the joint.

On Saturday mornings I was allowed to join them. The girls would wear flowing midi dresses or kaftans. We would have a head band across our forehead and paint freckles on our nose with brown eyeliner. We would put a flower or two in our hair; pick up our baskets filled with daisies and head off to the center of town. We would amble around the crowd randomly handing out daises saying "Have a nice day!"

I think the others got it into the flow a lot better as they were stoned compared to the very sober me. Our gestures weren't often appreciated as this was a period when the Rhodesian war was being fought and so our actions were deemed unpatriotic. It was a communal home and we all were assigned tasks thorough out the day as we were all contributing towards making a comfortable life for ourselves. I felt free and connected to life.

I enjoyed the life for about six months just drifting not having to make any decisions or plan ahead. I was living in the moment. Then I realized that this had just been a healing point I wanted more definition to my life. I wanted more and I knew that that special person, that elusive element, the final connection to me would not be found in my current environment. I had to move on. I found a job as a textile designer and moved into an apartment which I shared with two other women and got on with creating a new chapter in my life.

Photos of Steve and Beverly as teenagers. Clear Attitude.

Chapter Thirteen

China Town

Nothing is impossible the word itself says I'm Possible
– Audrey Hepburn

My Thursday's luncheons and part time work were "time fillers." I needed outside contact in order for the tumour not to consume my life and with Steve's loss of job it became more urgent for me to find a permanent position to work from. Steve never once asked me to work, he always said we would get by. He had cashed in some insurance policies in order for us to continue. I know that I need to find a base in order to feel more secure.

Singapore's Chinatown is the island's traditional Chinese quarters. The major attractions are shopping and eating. Antique shops abound, specializing in everything from large furniture and decorative pieces to small jewelry, porcelain and jade. Haggling, bargaining is the rule of the day with shopkeepers.

A friend had taken me to lunch at an esoteric center in China Town, in what had once been the red light district. The shop houses there had been turned into café, restaurants, karaoke pubs and massage shops. I had loved the atmosphere of the center, on the opposite side of the road was the café and book shop with a downstairs seating area where one could sit and glance through the books. It was full of people having coffee or one of the many health drinks on offer, a meeting point and discussion area. Across the road was the yoga center and consulting rooms where various practitioners could work from. My friend had told me that the owner was an Australian Greek lady called Stella. When she was discussing opening the café people asked her what she was going to name it. She would always dismiss the question with "whatever" and the name just stuck when she came to name the center. It was named Whatever.

I still had my company that I had set up but I was only working in the heart lands doing a bit of counselling there when I could. Although they had very little money they would always insist on giving me a small donation. I tried many times not to accept it until I realized that I needed to do so to save them from "loosing face". They needed to give and I needed to learn to accept but it was difficult.

Some of my old clients from Arab Street still requested that I help them. I would go to their homes but it was draining because once I went into their homes, I lost the professional aspect to my work. People act different when they are in their own homes as opposed to a professional office type environment.

One day, I was so exhausted, I had just been held "hostage" in the home of an old client. What should have been a one hour session turned into a grueling three hour brain drain for me. At the end when I had to be almost rude to get away, this very wealthy client said that she had not been to the bank that day so I could have a donation of all her small change she had in her bag. Counting up the small change she managed a handful of coins which amounted to a grand total of five dollars. I walked out of her home not knowing the area I was in, tears of frustration and exhaustion running down my face as I looked for a taxi to take me home. I thought about how imbalanced the world was; my gentle nurturing Thursday people who had nothing and yet gave me so much, not only insisting that I be given my fees but also looking after me. Here was a very wealthy person, just taking full advantage of me. I was exhausted and so emotionally spent.

Finally after much walking I managed to flag down a taxi. I asked him to take me home. Suddenly, out of nowhere I had a change of plan. I felt my fighting spirit restored as I asked the taxi driver to change direction and take me to Whatever cafe in China Town.

I arrived there with a throbbing headache and low spirit. I asked the receptionist if she knew of how I could apply to rent one of the counselling rooms to work from on a part time basis. She asked me to please sit down while she phoned the owner, Stella. She returned to me with a cup of tea and said the owner had asked me to please wait for her. She had gone home for the day but would return immediately to see me. She would be there in about fifteen minutes. While waiting I gazed around the little cozy restaurant and loved the ambiance, it felt good.

Stella whizzed in, the thing about Stella is that she never moved slowly. She started talking to me and asked me if I had seen the advert she had placed on the internet asking for a replacement counsellor. I replied I had not. She said that was amazing because she had described that she needed someone exactly like me. She commented that when she wrote the advert, she was knew she asking for a "tall order" but that I fitted the bill completely. She "hired" me then and there. Once again, I had to tell her about Steve and his illness and that I could only work part time. There would be days that I could not come into work. She was happy with that and so began my warm and wonderful days at Whatever.

Stella was larger than life, a big personality with a bigger heart. She had a no-nonsense approach to life and could at times be quite intimidating. She was outspoken and did not refrain from holding back any views. She would often be found sitting outside Whatever at one of the café pavement tables, smoking a cigarette and drinking a glass of wine. She had the policy that if life got too tough you just reverted to the three B's; A trip to Bali, A Bonk and some Booze.

Our weekly staff meetings were held on the floor of the yoga center, with Stella lying on the floor and the staff gathered around her. She had built up a lovely group with the staff she hired. Once I started working there, the staffs were wonderful and felt like "family". It took a lot of pressure off me. Angela the young secretary would ask what days and what times I was available and would do all my bookings for me so I just had to appear for duty. Stella was very well connected and so she introduced a lot of her "elite" friends to me and my old clients supported me once again. I had an amazing counselling room to work from.

The clients were so diverse and everyday was something new. I became counsellor to a well-known Singapore theater director and actress. She brought other young actresses who were struggling in all areas to meet me. We spent many happy hours seated on the floor in group counselling sessions. They became good friends and have remained so throughout my stay in Singapore.

They put on a very controversial play in Singapore. It was the story of Annabel Chong, who was born on May 1972, in Singapore. She attended a catholic school in Singapore and was academically gifted, she majored in Fine Arts. She became a pornographic actress and became famous after starring an adult film that was promoted as The World Biggest Gang bang in which she had sex with 251 men on a public stage. The tile of the play was 251. Singapore is a proud nation of many first qualifications worldwide and did not want to be associated with this first; particularly as the beginning if the play stated with shouting out all

Singapore's first achievements and ending with *"first gang bang by Annabel Chong!"*

Many of the public were angry and thought it very disrespectful. The young actresses were harassed for wanting to be part of it. On the opening night the actresses were extremely nervous. They asked me to be back stage to give them support and help with some calming exercises before and after they had been on stage. It was amazing to be part of it. The backstage bustled with activity, it was electric with the girls changing costumes and wigs and floating around among them were many Swarovski studded gigantic dildos of every size and colour which were used as stage props in the sex scenes.

- **Beverly** Cheryl Miles is a super star in Singapore. Actress, singer and radio presenter. A beautiful soul! The poster is from a controversial play they were in about a Singapore porn-star. As it was so difficult emotionally for the actresses I was back stage giving them support. An amazing time. They remain my special friends!
- **Cheryl Miles** Aww Bev! I dunno about superstar hahaha! We couldn't have done that play without YOU!!!! We were ALL so emotional every night! Hahah! Love you and miss you! Let's do a LEO LUNCH soon

Often Angela and I would rush off and go into China town and have lunch among the bustle and noise of the local food courts. Sarbinda, the dear financial director would make certain that come pay day, I was the first practitioner to receive my pay. If she thought I showed any sign of developing a cold or flu she would make copious honey and lemon tea. She was always the gentle nurturer. Steve would often go to Whatever with me after a treatment and we would be so exhausted. Sarbindar would close the shutters in the upstairs yoga room and place pillows on the carpeted floor and get Steve and me to lie down there. She would close the door, keep everyone out and then awake us a few hours later with one of her lemon and honey teas. People began to tease me as to why Steve and I spent so long alone in the yoga room, behind closed and guarded doors. If they had peaked in they would have seen a tired, physically and emotional battered couple getting some good sleep.

One morning as I was rushing through the market area of China Town on my way to work a monk dressed in an orange robe stood in front of me and dropped a red envelope into my carrier bag and smiling handed me his donation book.

I was annoyed at this forceful request but as I was in a hurry I took two dollars to give him as a donation. He said "No Ten Dollar!"

I put my two dollars back in my wallet and took his red envelope out of my bag and handed it back to him saying "No want!"

I started to walk away but the monk tried to put his hand in my carrier bag and was making all sorts of frantic gestures. Thinking I had met the mad monk, I started walking away as fast as I could. I could hear him pursuing me and calling out to me. I ran faster.

When I arrived home that evening, I told Steve about the strange mad monk I had met. I was mortified however when I was unpacking my carrier bag, a charm fell out. It had been inside the red envelop and this is what the monk wanted back. I often looked for him to return the charm but never saw him again.

Working at Whatever also had its share of problems in that it was situated on Keong Saik road. It had been a red light district in long gone days but still had a few dubious looking shops with women standing in doorways and asking passing men to come in for a "massage" between the cafes and art shops.

Taxi drivers in Singapore are friendly and love nothing better than a good chat along the drive. I think they need to keep talking in order to stay awake during their long taxi shift work. Often, I would get a shocked look when I would ask to go to Keong Saik road as it was a bit off the tourist route. The taxi driver would ask why I was going there and before I knew about its red light district, I would reply, "Because I work there".

So once I became aware of that I always went into a bit more detail of where I worked.

The name Whatever caused further problems for me when another taxi driver asked where I worked. I was busy texting on my phone so replied offhand, "Whatever".

There was total silence after that and I sensed a very angry attitude coming from him.

He then spoke up; "Excuse me Miss but you dismissed me when I was talking to you. Why would you do that?"

I was completely unaware of what he was talking about so I asked him.

He replied, "Well, you know when we get dismissal with our children when they ask too many questions, we get tired of giving answers and in the end we just say Whatever! Just now I asked where you work and you dismissed me by saying Whatever."

I quickly apologized and explained that I really did work at Whatever and made him pull up right under the sign of the center saying WHATEVER. I pointing to it and saying "You see that's where I work!" He laughed so much!

Steve was without a job and feeling ill after the impact of two radiation treatments. The only way we could stay on in Singapore was that Stella generously offered to become our local sponsor. Because of this we did not have to leave the country. Steve still had to have regular scans and the bill for his daily medication was huge. He still needed to see specialists for his eye sight and regular visits to the neurosurgeon. The medical bills were daunting and climbing, we could hardly keep up with them. He was so aware of the financial responsibility he still had towards his family. He wrote explaining our circumstances and that he would not be able to contribute that month but would catch up with double payments as soon as he had work. The reply he received was; "Don't use your tumour as an excuse make me feel sorry for you!" so that was not an option. He needed to find work quickly and that added more stress to his daily life.

Steve was so ill in bed and could hardly move. He spent most of the time lying in the darkened bedroom. His headaches intense and his body raked with pain. At this stage Steve had collected a whole lot of doctors, one doctor referring him to another because of the complicated issues associated with his tumour. He had seen four neurologists, two neurosurgeons, a professor at the neurological research intuition, three radiologist, a brain and spine surgeon, three headache and pain specialists, an endocrinologist and a doctor from a pain control clinic, apologies to the others who were not mentioned.

Steve had tried just about every type of medication, at one stage taking eight variations of pills every four hours. He had tried all kinds of promising lotions and potions. They had even injected him with Botox in an effort to stop the headaches. He had a bad reaction to the Botox. He was given

Tramodal. Xanax. Dormicum. Anarex. Codeine phosphate. Paracetomal. Neurobion. Naramig. Lexotan. Neurontin. Erythomicin. Phenoxybenzamine. Morphine. Epilim.Valium. Diazepan. Lorazepan. Disprin. Ciprobay. Voltaren. Synflex. Atenolol. Zomig. Alprazolam. Apo-amitriptyline and even Thalidomide, the list was endless. Massage, Chinese herbal medicine, Chiropractor, Lymph drainage, all sorts of weird and wonderful "treatments" yet nothing could alleviate the pain, in fact the medicine and treatments often left him feeling worse off than before as his body reacted very badly to some of the medication. No-one could come up with any answers besides that it was a rare kind of tumour and because of where it was situated it was totally unpredictable.

One of the top ranking neurosurgeons had told Steve he only had two years left at the most to live. He took out a plastic model of the brain and took it apart bit by bit and showed us exactly where the tumour was and that eventually it would kill Steve. It was totally convincing.

He also looked at the scan taken after Steve's second bout of radiation and said in his opinion the tumour had grown and Steve would need immediate radiation again not a day to waste. He said that Steve needed to get to the oncology department and present himself at once for radiation. We went to the level of the hospital where the oncology center was and presented Steve along with his scans. A young man, looking not much older than eighteen, looked at the scans then Steve. Getting the facts of Steve's tumour all wrong, he told us to wait while he got his superior and prepared the radiation room for Steve's immediate treatment. His superior walked in clinging to Steve's scans. There was a moment of stunned silence between Steve and I as the superior looked like a mad professor who had just stuck his fingers in an electrical socket. His thin wiry hair was standing on end and he deep thick lens glasses. He was holding the scans up at odd angles in order to get a clearer view. He told Steve to come through so that he could prepare him for radiation. I looked at my watch and said "Oh not today we have a very important meeting, we'll come back another time".

The mad professor wasn't about to let us escape that easily he said that he would hold onto Steve's scans for us until we returned. Steve said "no need for that" and reached out grabbed the scans. Together we ran out. We laughed so much on the way home, despite just being given a "life sentence" Steve could still find humour in the situation. The top ranking neurosurgeon's real name was an old English slang word for Penis, just as well because after that Steve always called him a Dick anyway.

Steve:

In the interim Bev had met the wonderful Stella. Stella was larger than life, an incredibly outgoing and generous person. By becoming our local sponsor she gave me that much need break in which to focus on looking for a new position. Bev was really enjoying working at Whatever, and I enjoyed going to meet her there when I was in the city. There was a tremendous team of people there, and the main thing is that even though Bev and I were going through tough times financially she had her spark back.

How did I feel about being told I had two years to live? I don't really remember, but it was not something I started stressing about. I had done some crazy things and held a few risky jobs over the years. I really thought I would not reach my fiftieth birthday, which was two years ahead. I had been told by a neurosurgeon and a radiology nurse that the tumour would kill me. Something kills all of us at some stage of our lives, so I really just kind of accepted it. I did not start writing a bucket list or getting my affairs in order. It was never about how to cope with impending death, it was about how to live. Most of the books and internet links I had read were about someone planning their death or making arrangements for it. I wasn't planning on dying, I was planning on living and Bev was determined I live too!

Chapter Fourteen
The Operation and wedding.

When you realize that you want to spend the rest of your life with someone, you want the rest of your life to start as soon as possible

– unknown.

Beverly:

Although, Steve was very worried about not having a job and having to contribute financially we were able to do so thanks to help from banks and maxing out credit cards. Steve also cashed in a few insurance policies he had, although not large sums it enabled us to live through the next two months. I was calm as I just knew we would be alright. As long as I totally trusted, something always happened to help us. I was just so thankful, that Steve was in a position to get some bed rest. Even though he was in pain and unable to sleep, he could still lay in a dark room and rest. His body was painful all the time and he had to sleep with constricting abdominal and leg bandages to help with his circulation as well as the oxygen tank was always nearby. I knew the circumstances were bad and that Steve stressed daily about the need for him to get out of bed to find a job but I was comforted by the fact that he was getting the time out his poor battered body and mind needed. He was exhausted.

Steve should have been getting or at least feeling a bit better with the bed rest but the symptoms were manifesting even worse. The doctors suggested a full body scan for Steve and they found a tumour situated on his adrenal gland. Three of the doctors seeing Steve converged and said that it was important Steve have it removed as soon as possible. It was a very dangerous operation as the doctors did not know what to expect. They did not know if it was cancerous or if it was in anyway linked to the brain tumour. The endocrinologist was very excited as he thought it may be a Pheochromocytoma. He immediately counted himself in on the team of doctors to operate, waving his fee just to be able to assist in the theater. He was of great assistance to Steve and me. One weekend when Steve's pain was very bad he met me at a chemist in town in order to make certain I got the required medication. The pain clinic doctor who was also an anesthetist was going to be part of the team. The Surgeon doing the surgery was a wonderful, warm and outstanding man. He was calm and confident.

Steve asked if it was necessary to have the operation as it would add hugely to our existing medical bills. The doctors were in no doubt it was urgently needed but told Steve the seriousness of it and that they could not offer any guarantees. They had no knowledge of what would happen after the tumour was removed. If it was in fact linked to the brain tumour it could cause further growth to it rather than a reduction. One of the doctors pulled a coin out of his pocket and told Steve it was a very serious operation and the chances were fifty-fifty. He held the coin up and said it's like asking this coin "heads or tails?"

Whereupon he flicked the coin into the air and caught it in his hand, saying "heads or tails? That is the kind of choice you have." At worst Steve could die and at best there could be a reduction in the symptoms he was having. Steve after a lot of convincing decided to go ahead with the operation.

We had been together for fourteen months. We were lying in bed one night, Steve and I having discussed the pros and cons of the operation. It was a scary decision he was making and he then said "Let's do it."

I thought he was talking about the operation but the tone was very different, a soft, vulnerable gentleness to it, so I asked him "Do what?"

He replied, "The thing, let's get married."

That moment so much happened in my mind at once elation, joy but also fear. I was so terrified that Steve would not survive the operation. I loved this man so much.

Two lots of plans were being made. The operation itself was not that simple. Steve would first have to have two weeks of block medication before the operation. This drug was called Phenoxybenzamine. Steve would have to gradually reduce all other medication and take this for two weeks before the operation. They would not consider removing the tumour and adrenal gland without the block medication because without it he could have an adrenalin rush that could cause an arrest within seconds. The surgeon was going to approach the adrenal glands through an incision in the abdominal wall, moving the bowel and other organs out of the way to gain access to the kidney and adrenals. As well as taking the medication Steve needed bed rest and to be kept calm.

Steve and I decided to have a quiet wedding in a register's office in Singapore. We were duly advised that in Singapore one was married by a Solemnizer. Little Lei, was the nurse assistant of one of the doctors and was such a support to me. Her gentle hugs were given when I needed them most. She had invited me to the wedding of her daughter. It was a great honour. It was a traditional Chinese wedding which takes the whole day to complete and consists of many different ceremonies. It starts with the groom going to the bride's house to fetch her. The bridesmaids stand outside the door and block him from entering until he has satisfied them with enough money or gifts. It's done in playful jest but the gifts are very real. Eventually when they think the groom has done well they allow him through. He then presents gifts to his wife's parents and they do a handing over ceremony. The bride is dressed beautifully in a heavily embroidered Chinese silk gown.

Once the handing over session is over, the groom takes his bride to his parents' home and here they have the tea ceremony. The eldest relative gets served first. So the new young bride will serve the grandmother tea from a special Chinese wedding tea set. The grandmother sat on an ornate chair placed in the center of the room. The bride went onto her knees head bowed and held the cup up high for the Grandmother to drink. The grandmother then blessed her with good comments. "My daughter how pretty you are!" "You will be the bearer of fine sons" and such like.

After that the grooms parents are both seated in the center of the room. Again the bride pours tea for each of them, kneeling before them, head lowered as she raises the cups to them. She first serves the father and then the mother. They also give blessings. Then the big moment arrives, the mother in law now stands up and she gives her new daughter in law a gift. Much meaning is placed upon the gift, the more expense the more you have the approval of your new mother in law. In this case there was huge admiration as the groom's mother placed a diamond necklace around her new daughter in laws neck. There is then lunch for everyone. Other people from the HDB apartments coming over to join in a communal lunchtime feast!

After lunch I headed home but it not the end of the wedding as there was a whole afternoon ahead of ceremonies and change of wedding gowns. The whole function escalated into the final huge formal dinner party in the evening. It is traditional that the wedding photos are taken weeks before the wedding. Everyone dresses up in their wedding apparel and goes to a local park or place of interest and have many photos done. This is done so that they can then be put on display at the wedding for the guests to look at and comment on.

When I confided to Lei that Steve and I were going to get married she was overjoyed. I told her we would just go to the Singapore registrar of marriages and get married there. She was fully aware of Steve's condition and so immediately replied..."No need, I will get the solomizier to come to your home and marry you there."

We had decided to keep it secret to avoid fuss. Our previous common law marriage had been hectic. We just wanted peace and quiet. I was radiantly happy and the Whatever group noticed this...I just couldn't contain the secret and burst out..."So Ok, we're getting married!"

That was followed by joyous screeches and hugs! Everyone shared in my happiness. I told Stella, about our plans to just have the solomizer around to the house and get it done that way.

A few days later, Steve and I received an invitation to a wedding....ours! Stella and Angela set about organizing it. They organized it from Whatever Yoga center and all Steve and I had to do was attend. Everything was done for us all in beautifully perfect detail. Stella loaned me one of her designer dresses. Invitations were given out. The solomiser booked. The date was set.

A strange coincidence was that Steve's friend, Brad called him from Dubai and said he would be in Singapore for the weekend, would it be possible to stay with us.

Steve said "yes, sure and by the way would you like to be my best man?"

Brad said "sure!"

The phone rang again a few minutes after Steve had put it down. It was Brad and he asked "You asked me to be your best man?"

Steve said "Yes, we are getting married."

Neena use to act in TV commercials and so every year she had her portfolio redone. One week before I got married she took me to her portfolio photo shoot. She asked that they take photos of me to give to my husband as a wedding gift. She explained that this was a very lucky thing to do to ensure that Steve and I have a long marriage. So I was done up, dressed up and photographed many times as everyone got into the excitement of the "bridal" photo shoot.

My Lucky Bridal Shoot photo.

We knew Steve would have to have the tumour and the adrenal gland removed soon after we got married. No doctor could give us any guarantees so we were both feeling extremely apprehensive but our forth coming wedding gave us something to focus on. The days leading up to the wedding had Steve and I practicing saying "solimiser" over and over again to perfect it, we were so scared in our nervous state we would slip up and say "Sodimiser" instead.

Before Steve and I got married I was required to go to our country's embassy to get our personal documents signed and verified. I also had letters from the doctors stating Steve's pending operation as the need for an urgent marriage. A member of staff was so horridly mean to me. She point blank refused to look at or sign any of our documents or read the accompanying doctors letter. She told me I was not to expect favours from her.

I asked "May I ask you one thing, if you wanted to could you sign the documents that we need in order to get married?"

She replied "Yes, I could but I won't!"

Everything shattered inside me in that moment; all Steve's treatments, the scary operation ahead, the unkindness I was subjected to. It just suddenly impacted on me and I started crying uncontrollably. Another member of staff took me to a chair outside her office. I was bawling, huge massive unable to hold back sobs with my mascara running down my checks.

Eventually someone came up to me and said if I bought Steve back with me the next day, the papers would be signed. I composed myself and said thank you very much and walked out. I went straight to the Singapore administrations and told them what had happened. They took my documents and had a small meeting. They came out and once again displayed their gentleness, compassion and kindness. They told me that they had decided in this case they would overlook the need to have our documents signed by our embassy and they would do the signing and verification themselves.

On the day of our wedding, I left the home early to get dressed at Whatever. When I arrived the place was a hive of activity as the yoga room was transferred into a beautiful venue for our wedding. As always Stella outdid herself. The ambiance she created was perfect, hundreds of candles their soft light glowing, photos of our children, the whole room full of fresh roses and jasmine. It was perfect.

The theater girls had decided to give me the gift of a wedding facial make up. They sent the stage theater make-up artist to do this for me. He was over the top "girlie" and theatrical. I was sitting in the yoga room when the door flew open and he flamboyantly asked where the bride was. He looked a bit disappointed when I announced I was in fact the bride.

We went through to my counselling room and the transformation began. There was no mirror and he worked away at my face and hair with great intensity for almost three hours. At last he pronounced he was satisfied with the results. He took me into the yoga room with its large full length mirror to take a look. I almost screamed out in horror! My face was pale, almost white with lots of black, black and more black around my eyes. Two red spots on my checks and my hair drawn up on top of my head and then with heavy set gel shaped to stand out in all directions. I knew if I stood close to someone they would stand a good chance of losing an eye. I looked like a bad geisha girl out of a horror movie. I kept the yell inside but saw the horrified looks on Stella and Angela faces. He announced with flourish that he had made me beautiful for my wedding. I could not tell him how horrified I was. I did not want him to lose face, so I thanked him for his time and asked if he would be staying for the wedding. To my huge relief he replied that he had another function to attend, I rushed him out of the door.

Then I yelled to Angela to get me some soap and shampoo. I only had fifteen minutes to go before the guests arrived. The yoga center had a shower and I ran to it in a huge panic as I scrubbed my face and washed out my hair. My skin was glowing red from the scrubbing and I just had time to wildly dry my hair and let it do its own thing before the guests arrived.

Stella, Angela and Loretta were my attendants. Loretta handed me pair of Swarovski earrings to wear. They were a gift from her and the theater girls. They matched my Stella gown to perfection. I wore them with pride. The curtain between the yoga center and the counselling rooms were closed and they would peep out and tell me which of the guests had arrived. There was great excitement and whoops when Steve arrived.

Stella and Lei were to be our witnesses'. The very serious solemniser called Steve behind the curtains where we had to choose our wedding vow words from a selection he held out, we chose the shortest. Then he and Steve went back into the yoga section and the solemniser solemnly announce the wedding was about to begin.

We were waiting on the other side of the curtain and Stella, Angela and Loretta each gave me a warm hug and told me it was time to make my appearance. They knew how I had longed for this day, so I teased them by turning around hands on hips and saying "Hum, think I changed my mind" whereby they laughing shoved me through the curtains and I went flying into the yoga area looking like a very eager bride indeed.

Angela giving me the shove.

The wedding was magical. I flew out from behind the curtain and the first people I saw were Linda and her husband John sitting in the front row. Linda's calm presence was so reassuring. I walked up to Steve waiting for me, his blue eyes encompassing me and letting me know I was simply where I was meant to be. We put our arms around each other and arm in arm recited our vows. The love and energy in that room was tangible and everyone felt it. We have often been told that it was a wonderful wedding because each and every one of the guests had so wanted to be there and share in our joy. We smiled our way through the ceremony but my voice broke and tears welling up in my eyes when I said the phrase "till death do us part". There wasn't a dry eye in the house as all our guests knew that Steve had his dangerous operation ahead.

Now you will feel no rain
For each of you will be a shelter for the other
Now you will feel no cold
For each of you will feel the warmth of the other
Now you will feel no more loneliness
For each of you will be a companion to the other
Now you are two persons
But there is one life before you
Go now to your dwelling place
To enter into the days of your life together
And may your days be good and long upon this earth.
Apache Wedding blessing.

Our friend Nicola gave us our own star in the sky. Registered in the international star registry **as Beverly& Steve Cygnus Ra21h31m30.66s D32 8'39.59"**

Steve & Bev

Cheryl Miles Loretta Chen, Amy Cheng and Cynthia lee Macquarrie Background to the wedding photo is an autographed poster from The production 251

Bev with Amy, Loretta, Cynthia

Steve

It was strange how here we were in a foreign country, asking for assistance from our country's High Commission, and being refused out of sheer spite. Then approaching the Singaporean Registrar of Marraiges who went out of their way to assist us. It was quite incredible how helpful, friendly and efficient they were. It was as though they were happy for us as well.

Brad arrived a couple of days early and we had a few good days chatting about the old days when we worked together in Dubai. He had been very surprised to learn that I was getting married but once he met Bev she met with his approval. On the morning of the wedding we took a cab down to Whatever and were greated with great exciment by the waiting guests and we relaxed while waited for the proceedings to start.

The solemnizer took things very seriously. We had to go back-stage with him to run through the proceedings with him again. I was just battling to keep myself from smiling at the extreme seriousness with which he approached the whole business, and how it contrasted with the happy atmosphere generated by Stella, her team, and our guests.

Brad and I stood waiting for Bev to emerge from behind the curtains in the Whatever yoga centre. Next thing she basically came flying out from behind them. Seems she got a bit of encouragement from Stella and the girls. Bev looked stunning and radiant. Then in a couple of minutes it was over and we were married at last. And it felt good. It had taken a lifetime journey to find my sense of belonging and with Bev I had finally arrived home.

I was amazed at the number of people who attended the wedding. I don't know where Stella got the guest list from but my friends and collegues were there as well as every person Bev had ever helped in Singapore. The room was filled with genuine shared joy and happiness. Most of the guests knew that I would be going for a surgery that I might not recover from but they made sure the focus was on the moment. Life, joy, happiness and shared laughter.

Looking around at the diversity of the guests I felt so proud of Bev because not only had she taken care of me twenty four hours a day in often stressful circumstances but she had still managed to nurture and give hope to so many other people and the guests were a testimony to this.

CHAPTER FIFTEEN
Fifty-fifty

Believe you can and you're halfway there
– Theodore Roosevelt.

Beverly:

A week after our wedding Steve received a call asking him to go for a job interview that Sunday. Being asked for an interview on a Sunday should have been a warning sign to the eccentricity of the person, but it was an answer to a prayer. It was a huge drop in position and salary for him but it was a job. No-one in business circles knew Steve had a brain tumour. We were not being deceptive at all. We knew from past experience that most people associate brain tumours with mental illness. The minute you mention "brain tumour" the person you are talking to becomes uncomfortable.

Steve now had a job with a local company and his new boss was somewhat erratic and eccentric. Steve would often go to work in the morning and I would not see him for a few days again as his "boss" would decide to travel into neighboring Malaysia without any notice. Steve would always be required to have his passport with him. If he commented that he did not have any change of clothing with him and the boss would say never mind we will buy you some there. Steve would be taken away on a business trip immediately. He would disappear into the wild interior for up to three days at a time. Business would involve stopping over at family homes for a quick meal and staying in all kinds of weird and wonderful places. Steve got an education into local living and travelling. It was a family business and chaos ruled.

The company had its twenty fifth anniversary. Everyone was invited and the dress code was to dress in the traditional dress of the country you come from. South Africa has eleven different official languages and many more cultures. Steve and I decided to dress as we normally do to represent of "sector" of South African culture. I thought that maybe I could wear an African print dress to make it look a bit more authentic. I set about to search for an African print dress in Singapore after many days of searching I found one that would do. Unfortunately, it had a very low and revealing neck line. I bought it anyway and decided to take it to one of the many tailors in China Town and have her change the neckline to a more modest one. I told her it was needed urgently and I would return the next day for it.

The next day, I dashed off during my lunch hour from Whatever and tried the dress on. The top was dreadful; it was all ill-fitting, lumpy, out of shape and awful. I had paid in full and there are no money returns in Singapore. I arrived back at Whatever in tears. Stella took one look at the dress and told me to follow her. We did a brisk walk back to the dress maker. Stella confronted her with "You know it's a terrible job, you know me and my friends who support you. You are not doing right by this lady, give her money back now!"

To my amazement, she did. The shop had filled up with people who were all listening and then Stella turned round to me and on top of her voice said; "You know Bev, this is actually all your fault just because you were too scared to show a bit of tit!"

It still led to the problem of what to wear and again Stella had the perfect solution; borrow one of her designer gowns. Which I did and should have done in the first place, it would have saved a lot of bother. So I went to the function wearing a "Stella Gown" and showing quite a bit of "cleavage", enough to get me clinging to my shawl all night.

Steve was tired and physically drained of energy, working with the new company was erratic. He was still battling with all the effects of the tumour and the two radiations and awaiting his operation to have the adrenal gland and tumour removed. He had gathered about him a wide range of doctors who gave him a large amount of medication to ease their section of specialty in the tumour. Steve was clearly not coping physically. When he was not working he spent most of the time laying in our darkened bedroom, in an effort to block out the mind blowing headaches. However he could not sleep, no matter what he tried, meditation and so much more, sleep evaded him, days and nights without sleep. He just lay in bed, his body wracked in pain, his head throbbing and his hyperactive head activity.

I could do nothing to help and knew that the best course of action was to let Steve work through it himself and just provide the support he needed. These were the times I felt the isolation and aloneness the most. I would take many lone walks along East Coast Park looking at "ordinary people" in the park, wondering why their lives seemed so uncomplicated and easy. I would stand looking out at the ships in the ocean, the sea breeze blowing through my hair and I would cry at how unfair life was. I tried never to show Steve how much the tumour drained at my very soul and ate away my energy. I tried never to show the tears. I would not allow myself to break down but I did allow myself the luxury of a few tears shed alone.

Then I would breathe and resolve to fight stronger and harder, the tumour would not win. I could never reveal to Steve just how much the tumour ate away at me. This is what his main concern had been when I moved to join him in Singapore. I never once, even in the darkest phases of the tumour ever wanted to be anywhere but beside him. It was where I belonged.

The endocrinologist, the anesthetist and The Surgeon decided that if Steve was going to have the operation done, he needed to do it soon. This would involve a lot of preparation. Steve would first have to have a gradual reduction of all his medications. This lead to many stops and starts as Steve's whole system reacted badly to the reduction of the medication he needed. They would have to put him back onto the medication but lower the doses or introduce substitutes for it. His was always in pain and with the tampering of the meds all kinds of new symptoms were manifesting along with old. Steve was in agony at all times and he was working in the erratic and unpredictable job so he had no routine he could plan his day around or moments when he could just rest up for a few minutes. He eventually told the company that he was going for an operation and needed two weeks off.

While the medication was being reduced, the block medication Phenoxybenzamine needed to be slowly introduced into Steve's system before the Adrenal gland and tumour could be removed. Once again, Steve's stubbornness came to the fore. Steve had previously had a bad experience in hospital when he had to share a "ward" with another patient. It was a tiny room that could barely hold one bed let alone the two that were squashed in almost together with a thin curtain separating them. Steve's bed was against the window and the other patients bed was next to the bathroom they needed to share. Steve tolerated the sharing of the bathroom and the fact that he was right up against the bright light steaming in from the window, despite his sensitivity to light. Until the patient's family and friends started to arrive, a constant stream of visitors who arrived in a crowd and stayed all day. In Singapore most hospital visiting hours are from 8am to 8pm. It was a great social gathering; they sat on the bed and floor and covered every surface of the room. They peeked through the thin curtains separating the beds and talking quite openly about Steve. They commented about what they thought could be the reason for his stay in hospital. They brought in pots of food and all ate together, nosily laughing and talking. Steve could not use the bathroom when he needed to as the visitors used it. They even washed the after meal dishes in there too. Due to the tumour Steve had a massive intolerance to light and noise so the situation was a nightmare for him. Steve could not be moved as the hospital was full. He swore that if he ever went into hospital again it would only be if he could have a private room all to himself.

When all the arrangements were being made, Steve requested that I ask the surgeon to arrange a private room for him. The surgeon replied that he would see what he could do but he couldn't promise anything. I relayed this to Steve, he replied that was not good enough and that unless he was guaranteed a private room, he would not take the block medication. The surgeon laughed when I told him. But after a few days when Steve had still not began taking his block medication, the Surgeon realized just how serious he was. He guaranteed one for Steve. With that knowledge, Steve began taking his block medication. He experienced bad reactions to it, the sweats and shaking got worse as well as chronic headaches but there was no way the operation could be done unless Steve had taken it so he preserved.

Steve had to be in hospital the night before the operation for his preparation. Strangely enough, although the doctors had warned us about the dangers of this operation and the fact that Steve might not survive it, Steve and I did not talk about what to do should he not survive. We had no needs for words, we knew what each other was thinking and feeling. It did not erase the deep fear that I felt.

Steve was still going on about "they better have a private ward for me, otherwise I am going home!" on the way to the hospital. When we were shown to his room we burst into laughter. The surgeon had outdone himself, Steve had a private suite. It had a day bed for me to catch up on some sleep. The room was tucked away in the corner far away from any other outside sounds.

Steve was settled in and was grumpy at the immediate pocking and prodding going on with his body as the monitors and tubes were inserted. When left him that evening to go home and get some sleep before I was to return to the hospital in the morning, he was in his usual wide awake state.

When I arrived at the hospital at 6am, Steve's room was already a hive of activity. Each of the attending doctors did their own "inspections" and gave their instructions. When at last Steve was ready for theater, the nurses let me to walk at the side of the gurney as they pushed him to surgery. We held hands tightly all the way. I couldn't talk because I just wanted to throw myself across Steve and shout "Stop!" I felt that any minute I would break down with uncontrollable sobs. I could only imagine how Steve was feeling, yet he was joking with the staff and making them laugh.

They allowed me to go into the theatre with Steve. The anesthetist was already there. They transferred Steve to the operating table and then called me to say goodbye to him. We kissed and held our hands so tightly together. I couldn't bring myself to break away. Steve knew this and released me and with the most beautiful smile said "see you soon!"

The activity around Steve was frantic as they began to prepare him for the operation so as I walked out of the theatre door I did not get a last look at him. I knew I had to be brave but it was so hard. The endocrinologist walked by me and stopped and told me to be strong. Then the surgeon arrived and before he went into theatre he reassured me as much as he was able to. He told me to be brave and strong and that the operation would take about four hours. After that Steve would need to go straight to ICU. He asked me to stay close to the theater door at all times because if Steve's life was in danger or he did not recover they would let me in immediately. Those were the longest four hours of my life. I did not move away from the door for one second. I was terrified and silent tears just ran but I couldn't give vent to them. I prayed, begged, pleaded. I alternated between sitting on the floor and standing at the door. Although the doctors were operating, they thought of me waiting outside and sent a nurse aid out to give me a few progress reports on how the operation was going. Finally she said, "The operation is going well, it will only be about another half hour."

I couldn't celebrate yet, I just needed so badly to see Steve.

The endocrinologist was out first a smile on his face as he hugged me he said the operation had gone well. Then the Surgeon walked out a Big Smile on his face, he called me over and told me that Steve was truly remarkable, the operation had gone so well that Steve would not even have to go into ICU but instead would go to the recovery room before being taken to his private room. He said "He is calling for you! We are just getting him ready to move and he will be out in a few moments."

The anesthetist walked out also beaming and said it had gone so well. He apologized to me for the fact that I was told all the details of what could go wrong but he explained it had been a very serious operation and so I needed to be prepared for the worst. I thanked him.

The theater doors swung open as Steve's bed was pushed out. He was searching for my face and gave me a sleepy lopsided grin and took my hand like he would never let it go. I walked beside the bed as it was pushed to the recovery room. I stood outside and waited while they put Steve onto the recovery bed. When they called me in he was attached to monitors and had drips going into both arms and his neck. The worse thing was he was lying under a glaring white light and he had a chronic headache. I wanted him to be moved and settled in his private room so that he could be made comfortable. After a few hours he was moved. The day bed had been made up for me next to Steve's bed and we both feel into a deep sleep.

Steve spent a week in the hospital. The endocrinologist was extremely disappointed that the tumour had not been a Pheochromocytoma. One week later Steve and I saw his huge sense of his disappointment, as we sat in his office we saw a study chart on his wall. It was his presentation of Steve Williams' Pheochromocytoma. It was now something he was unable to present. The operation had been a disappointment for Steve too as it had not relieved any of the symptoms. The tumour that was removed was in no way related to the brain stem tumour. Steve was in a lot of pain and recovery was very slow.

We gave up our apartment in the condo block and eventually found a small apartment in a block of flats. It was tiny and we hired four people to help me clean it up. We had to give away a lot of our furniture as it would just not fit. We moved in and made it as cozy and homely as we could. We only used public transport as Steve could not drive due to the tumour and its effect on his coordination and eye sight. He had lost a lot a lot of confidence. The condo block we had moved into had a swimming pool and Steve would love to just emerge his body in the water and swim lengths in an effort to stay fit.

We laugh because it happens with such regularity that I say Steve must have some kind of special attraction aura. He can sit in a restaurant at a table far away all by itself and the tables around him will fill up even though there is plenty of space across the room. If anyone visits our home it's always Steve's favourite chair they are attracted to. It's even that way in car parks he will park his car far away from any other vehicle only to have Vehicles parking around his despite the empty spaces elsewhere. So it was frustrating for Steve as the condo swimming pool would be empty and he would want to catch a quick lone swim but within minutes of him getting into the pool it was filled with other people joining him.

Steve:

The call came at about 4pm on a Saturday afternoon. I answered my mobile phone and could not figure out what was being said as the caller was speaking so fast. I eventually got him to slow down enough to understand what he was saying. He said he had heard that I was "in the market' and I had lots of experience in what his company did and I must come and see him now. I was having a really bad day health-wise so told him I was busy. He said okay, gave me his address and told me to be at his office on Sunday afternoon at 2pm. Such was my introduction to the wonderfully eccentric RL!

The taxi drove past the rig-building shipyards on the way to my interview and I felt at home. This was where I came from and I wanted to be back. I was suddenly filled with enthusiasm and had not even had the interview. I met RL. He was all over the place conversation-wise. When I was in Dubai I was working for a company that did what RL's company did, so within minutes RL was discussing my offer. The position was Offshore Engineering Manager and came with a drop in salary of about thirty percent of my previous position. I told RL I would think about and let him know in about an hour. I went home and discussed it with Bev. We agreed that despite the drop in salary I would accept the position regardless. I needed to be working as soon as possible. I called RL and informed him of my decisions. He told me to be at the office at 8am the next morning.

And so began one of the wackiest and funniest times I have ever had in a company. RL and his wife VL had started the company together about twenty five years back and had succeeded, against all odds, in turning the company into a successful venture. RL was all over the place all of the time taking on mad-cap offshore construction projects, whilst VL ran her division very well, which ensured that RL's odd projects were always funded, despite his occasional "mistakes". He was the only person I have ever come across who could cost out an entire offshore accommodation and construction barge on the back of a cigarette box in five minutes. Awesome!

No day working with RL was the same. He would come into my office at 5pm on a Monday afternoon and say "Come, we're going to the yard". Five minutes later we would be driving up to the company's shipyard in Lumut, Malaysia – a six hour drive away. I would give Bev a call and say I would see her whenever. We would meet his "business associates" at a golf club in Kuala Lumpur. He would introduce me in a slightly derogatory term for a Caucasian in Mandarin, but then tell them that I was okay though! The he would book me into the worst hotel he could find whilst he went and stayed at his mother's house – a wonderfully regal lady. We would be on the road at 5am the next morning, stopping for "makan" at the Ipoh market, before heading down to Lumut. RL was always testing me to see how I would react to these little things, but I just cruised and enjoyed the experiences.

We would work like crazy for several days in Lumut and suddenly Robert would be shouting that we had to go, and off we would be back on the road to Singapore. I am not a great one at talking too much when driving for hours at a time and nor was RL, so we would drive back in silence apart from when one us wanted a pit stop. RL needed to recruit an Internal Engineering Manager and asked if I knew of anyone. A friend of mine from Dubai was in the market as he had just come off contract so I recommended him to RL. RL employed him and TK came to join us in Singapore. One week RL wanted TK to go with him to the Lumut yard. TK likes to chat so tried to get a conversation going with RL. RL came straight back at him and said "No time for idle chit-chat, need to do much thinking while driving'! TK thought he was off his rocker.

It was whilst working for RL that the doctors picked up the tumour on my adrenal gland. After much discussion and debate with the doctors and my radiologist they decided that perhaps the removal of the tumour might alleviate some of my symptoms. The endocrinologist was really excited as he suspected it may be a Phaeochromocytoma – an extremely rare type of tumour that he had never come across before. He even started planning a lecture on it to present to his peers. I really felt for him after the biopsy showed it was not as he had already booked the lecture room at the hospital and was advertising his "find".

On the morning of the operation a person entered my room and told me they were there to shave me. I was unable firstly to figure out what sex this large hairy person was, and secondly if they were operating on my chest why did I require a full-body shave? Anyway the shave took place and they came in with a gurney and wheeled me out into an elevator and down into the bowels out of the hospital where the operating theatres were. I could not understand what all the hysterics were all about and told them I could stand and walk to the theatre. Not a chance! They take these things very seriously in Singapore.

They left me on the gurney in a corridor outside the operating theatre and administered a pre-op sedative. I was lying there with my eyes closed when I felt the sheet covering my naked body being lifted. I opened my eyes and saw a nurse having a good look at my private parts. She quickly dropped the sheet and scurried off. This happened twice more in the next five minutes and I started getting a bit ticked off. When I felt yet another person start lifting the sheet I reached down and grabbed their hand, opened my eyes to see one of the hospital receptionists standing there, trying desperately to get free from my grip. I told her I did not think she should be doing that, and released her hand and watched her run down the corridor. I thought it was quite amusing.

The doctors involved had warned me that this was an extremely dangerous operation and at best my chances of surviving it were fifty-fifty. I could cope with that fact but it was difficulty seeing Bev trying to cope emotionally with the fact that it might be the last moment we saw each other. They allowed Bev to go into the theatre with me. The anesthetist was already there. They transferred me to the operating table and then called Bev to say goodbye to me. We kissed and held our hands so tightly together. It was difficult for Bev to break away; I realized this and released her hand, smiled at her and said "see you soon"!

The activity levels in the theatre got a bit frantic as they began to preparing me for the operation. Bev told me later that as she walked out of the theatre door she did not get a last look at me due to all of the people in the room. Bev knew she had to be brave and she said it was so hard. The endocrinologist stopped Bev on her way out and told her to be brave but to expect the worst.

As Bev left the theatre they placed me on a contraption of a bed that I had never seen before. No sooner was I on the bed that it started opening out and I was left lying there with my arms and legs spread-eagled out, stark naked. My wonderful surgeon Dr. R came and stood between my naked spread-eagled legs and explained the procedure. It did feel rather uncomfortable. Then the anesthesiologist pushed the play button and the room was filled with religious hymns. He then did his bit and I went to sleep.

I awoke freezing cold, naked on an air-mattress of some kind with a bright light above me. I started shivering like I had never done before. Someone came over, placed a blanket over me and pushed a button that started blowing warm air into the air-mattress. Something I can never understand about hospital recovery rooms is how bright they keep them. I would rather come to in a slightly dim room with no noise. This was just the opposite – bright lights and so much noise. They told me I was in the Recovery Room. I had been told I would be in ICU for at least three days, but I had apparently come through the operation so well that they decided to put me in the Recovery Room for a few hours and then transfer me to my ward.

I lasted a week in hospital before insisting they let me go home. They wanted me in hospital for at least two weeks and then at home in bed for another two. I checked myself out, spent a week in bed at home and then went back to work.

Local companies in Singapore are pretty harsh on their employees, and it was the same at RL's. The morning I reported back the company financial manager came into my office and asked for my hospital bill. I told her I had given them a letter from my doctor as well as a medical leave certificate so why did they require the bill as well. She replied that anyone could forge such documents and if I did not give them a verified copy of the bill I would not get paid for the period I was off. They got their copy.

Chapter Sixteen

Coping skills

Don't be afraid to stand up for what you believe in;
even if it means standing alone

- unknown

Beverly:

It was awful for us to learn on the report of Steve's next scan that he needed to have a third series of radiation treatments. It was so cruel because both Steve and I had truly believed that the radiation would make the tumour disappear and our lives would be normal once more. Life without the tumour had been the goal. Hope was dashed each time.

I had to work while Steve went for his checkup brain scan. He was called to receive his scan by a young nurse who told him that she had looked at the scan. She stated that the tumour had grown and it was going to kill him. I was furious that she had done that. We took the reports to Steve's neurologist who said that Steve would need more radiation. It was a huge blow to us. So once again, Steve went to mornings of radiation treatments and then going straight to work afterwards.

Steve was totally exhausted. He began seeing other neurologists, doctors and health workers, looking for any new possibilities or treatments. Steve was on many different meditations, they would work for a time and then symptoms would change. It was an ongoing fight for him against the pain. Life was a spiral of hopes being dashed as we went from one doctor to another in the hope of finding some answers. I lost myself in my work and going on long isolated walks where I would cry out my frustration as Steve tried to block out pain and deal with it in his own way. We had agreed to this in the beginning of the treatments, it had to be done Steve's way. He always had a strong gut feel, an instinctive feel for what would work for him and what wouldn't. This related to the many doctors he saw at this time too. We named the all, Dr nasty, Dr Happy, Dr Fool, Dr Crazy one, Dr Weird and so on as the list became impressive. From the very beginning Steve knew it was not what the doctor said but what he felt about the information he received within himself that would matter the most.

It was hard to see Steve battling to deal with the pain. He had his own sense of aloneness and isolation. I could be there, walking besides him and being supportive but I had to let him find his way, it was his struggle. We only knew that being together made us stronger and united all the fragmented pieces we had become. Together we could survive anything.

Aloneness and isolation had always been a part of my world and had given me the strengths that I now needed in order to cope. I had got married four days after my eighteenth birthday. I was living in Bulawayo Rhodesia and at that time it was very much the thing to do. Rhodesia had declared UDI from British rule and the war against terror had started. All the young males were required to do military training on leaving school for a period of nine months after which they then did continuous call up. This was a period of six weeks in the bush followed by ten days R & R (rest and recuperation). It was a time of no guarantees, life was short. Many of my friends lost boyfriends and husbands to the war. Most of the women married young like I did and learnt to live alone to the monotony of life broken by the six week cycle of R&R.

We were young wives and mothers at the home front. R & R was the trigger of many pregnancies that were encouraged to ensure an ever growing population. The men too felt happier and safer leaving pregnant wives behind.

Shortly after getting married we moved to Beit Bridge, where my husband worked on an open cast mine. The site was thirty five miles from Beit Bridge on a long and bumpy dirt road through the bush. He was still doing regular army call ups between work. He was now put into a different unit that required him to be in the bush for six weeks followed by three months at home.

The mine was in the middle of a valley and in a busy area of terrorist activity. The army had moved some of its regular force into the area and used the mine as its base. They decided that as many of the women were often alone we needed to be trained in the art of shooting in case we ever needed to do so. The first time and only time I used the FN rifle was when they gave it to me to shoot at target practice. I only succeeded in landing heavily on my bottom. I had no idea where the bullet had gone certainly not directed at the target. I would not touch one again but learnt to become a good shot with a point 22 rifle, which was positioned next to my bed.

I had my first son by this time and was very pregnant with my next when I decided I could no longer live in the bush. It was fine when I was alone but having children to protect made it more dangerous and scary. There were always reports of attacks on isolated farms, rapes and terrible unspeakable atrocities.

The end came for me when we had dug out shelters built outside our back doors, deep holes surrounded by sand bags. With our men away we had regular meetings about what we should do in emergencies as the mine was in a valley they expected it to be mortared. I had baby of sixteen months old and was heavily pregnant with my next. I was told if we were ever attacked to pull the mattress off the bed and climb into the bath with my son and then pull the mattress over us. All this before the mortar hit the house? I thought that an impossible task for anyone let alone a heavily pregnant mother carrying a toddler.

One night when I was alone with my son, the alert went off and with it the electricity shut down. In the dark, I grabbed my son and terrified I ran, ran and ran about three long blocks away in the dark to a neighbor's house. I stayed there for the night but decided I needed to move to the relative safety of a town. So we moved back to Bulawayo.

With my husband doing continuous call ups I learnt to cope with and do things on my own. Even childbirth was a very lone experience with him being away on call up. I had three sons in quick succession. Life involved meeting up with friends and forming play groups for our multitude of children and waiting.

It was only when the war was lost that the cycle was broken and most young men who had been actively involved chose to leave the country rather than face any backlash from the new government. We left and moved to South Africa. We moved to a town where my Gran lived and we were reunited again.

Bev and her three sons.

Steve in his unit.

Steve:

I was disappointed to hear that I required yet another treatment but felt that I had two already; so let's just get on with it and get it over and done with. I was angry with the young nurse who told me the tumour was going to kill me and mentioned it to the cashier as I was paying for the scan. Within minutes the senior partner of the practice called me on my mobile phone, apologizing profusely. I later found out that if I had reported it to the Medical Council in Singapore there would have been dire consequences for the practice, but why would I do that? I had a tumour and yes, it might just kill me. I just did not like being told it would.

I realised I had reached the third level of Grief – Bargaining. I would speak to whichever higher being there was and say "if you cure me I will …." Anything that came into my head. It did not last long as I am a realist and one does not bargain in such a way. Life does not work that way. Time to get on with it. That had always been my approach to life.

Back in Rhodesia I was finishing my A Levels and was going to university to study Architecture – a long way away from the toxic environment that was my home life that I could not wait to leave. Being a South African living in Rhodesia I was not conscripted into military service like the rest of my friends were. A group of us were sitting having a few beers in a local pub one afternoon – a sort of farewell now that school was behind us and we would all be going our separate ways, when I had another of my "brain-waves". I announced to my friends that I was going to enlist. They all laughed and told me I was crazy.

I left them and drove to the nearest enlistment centre where I asked a Sergeant how I could enlist. He asked me if I had been drinking. I mentioned that I had a few beers with friends. He politely told me to piss off and come back when I was sober. I was back there at 8am the next morning in front of the same Sergeant. He sat me down and gave me a lecture as to the dangers of enlisting in a country that was at war, and it was not my country and not my war. I told him had been living there for several years so it was basically my country, and my war. He wearily asked me which branch I wanted to volunteer for and pushed the forms across the table.

I joined the British South Africa Police Force Support Unit. The "Unit" as it was called had developed from an old police askari unit into a slick fighting force. This was the unit that many of my friends were joining so I thought it logical to join and be with them. I then drove to Santa the barber and asked him to shave off my shoulder length hair as I was joining the army. He looked at me as though I was crazy and told me in a Portugese profanity that I was basically a stupid idiot with no father. When he finsihed I paid him the required twenty five cents, and as was custom with Santa he handed over a condom.

I drove into our yard and my mother came out the front door. She took one look at my bald head and started screaming and slapping at me. She tried her hardest to get the police to rescind my enlistment, but it was all to no avail. A week later I left home and reported for basic training.

Basic training was not fun. Our instructors thought that the meaning of fitness was being a marathon runner, so all we did was run. Having being a swimmer throughout school running was not one of my strong points so I did battle a bit with that part of it. Our instructors were tough, no-nonsence guys and physical beatings as punishment for some supoposed infrigement were the order of the day. We had some officers from the South Africa military who came to observe us in training for a week. Their comment on our training when they left was that it was "Brutal". So starts a man's education.

Suddenly basics were over and we were assigned to our troops across the country. The day after basics I left to join Sierra troop in the north of the country. Our basic role was recon and observation, tracking, and follow-up after an incident. We would be operational in the bush for six weeks at a time, return to the city for a week's R n R (Rest and Recuperation), then three days at "Battle Camp" to sweat the booze of R n R out of you, and then the troop would be deployed for another six weeks. After a while the units was reorganised into companies and I became an officer in Alpha Company.

R n R was always a welcome break. A friend of mine had a thirty foot yacht at lake Kariba, a few hours drive away from Salisbury. Four of us friends would regularly pile into his car and head for the lake. We'd fill the yacht with cases of Castle Beer and fishing bait, and sail across to Sanyati Gorge, where we would spend a week fishing, spearfishing and just chilling out. It seemed strange to some of our other friends who just wanted to let rip in town, partying in the clubs, and generally having a wild time. The four of us found the solitude of Kariba therapeutic after a hectic and tense six week deployment. Each to their own.

I really enjoyed my time in the Unit. Especially being in the bush. The best times were when we operated in far distant wildlife areas. Sitting quietly in a hide observing a track or village one would suddenly see some form of wildlife walk across in front of you, totally unaware you were there. Awesome stuff.

War is never pleasant for those innocent victims who get caught in the middle, nor is it for those families of the members of the military who become casualties of war. The guy who bunked next to me during basics was killed in action a week after being deployed, and so it went on.

When in our bush-camps, which were usually deserted farm houses that we set up a temporary base out of, the highlight was the arrival of the weekly mail pouch. It was not something that greatly excited me, but for many of the guys it was their link with the real world and they would gather excitedly in anticpation of a letter from home. By watching the faces of the guys who received mail one could tell who had reveived their "Dear John" letters from the wives or girlfriends. It was not pleasant watching a top operator going back to his tent with his shoulders heaving and tears in his eyes. That was part of war but one did not want to be on the next patrol with that person as you knew his mind was elsewhere.

Besides enjoying being in the bush and the camaraderie in the unit, it taught me an incredibe amount about man-management. Being an eighteen year old officer, second in command in a company of a hundred men, all experienced professional military men, who knew all the tricks of the trade, one earns one's stripes very quickly. The experience of serving with those men served me well in terms of man management skills in later years as my career developed.

Suddenly after two years it was over and I was a civilian again, apart from still being called up for regular camps as the war continued. It was difficult adjusting to civilian life again, and I saw how some of my friends' lives went downhill over the years as they tried. There are still a lot of lost souls out there living in the past. Sad.

CHAPTER SEVENTEEN

Psychedelic becomes reality.

Learn to love what you have been taught to fear
– Felix Baumgartner.

Beverly:

Steve had slipped into deep depression mostly caused by lack of sleep. He stayed in the dark room and his body was full of endless pain, continuous pain and medications that did not work. Enter Dr Crazy; he was a neurologist specializing in pain control. He had another theory on Steve's pain. He thought that it was caused by the years of medication Steve had been taking. He would put Steve into hospital remove all his medication, everything in one go and then he would slowly introduce different medications to check which ones worked for Steve and which ones did not. It sounded so plausible and a good solution in theory but we did not realize the danger of putting that into practice.

Once again, Steve was placed into hospital. On this occasion he was given a private room. He was put into bed where immediately he was given drips and all medication was stopped. With the withdrawal of medication the pains became intense. Every single symptom that he had fought returned with twisted nightmarish pain. He was not allowed any food or drink, all he had was a saline drip. He spent two days in agony while his body was "cleared" of all medication. This was equivalent to going "cold Turkey" His body crying out for some form of relief from the pain of withdrawal. Steve went to the quiet place within himself and just allowed the pain to wash over him in continual waves. I would go to the hospital in the morning, rush to work and then back home to have a shower and rest before evening hospital visit. It was awful leaving Steve alone but I also knew he needed the "space" to deal with the pain. The third day he was declared drug free and now they would begin to introduce new drugs to see what worked and what didn't. He had several drips going into each arm.

The nurses were all very tiny and sat behind a huge counter at the nurses station so that just their eyes could be seen over it. The mother superior would visit Steve each evening and say a benediction for him. The atmosphere was warm and loving. They always made sure that when I was with Steve I had a cup of tea and biscuit.

One evening, I left Steve later than usual to go home. He was very uncomfortable and agitated, the nurse explained that it was the introduction of the different medication but everything was under control. I was so exhausted that I could not remember my home address when the taxi driver asked me where I wanted to go. I could only say, "Drive East and I can show you where to go".

I searched through my handbag for an envelope or anything with my address on it but could find nothing. Once we got to the area in the east where our apartment was located in I suddenly remembered but it was a very scary moment for me.

I showered and got into bed and then I began to laugh at not being able to remember my address. When I had first arrived in Singapore I had ventured out on my own to an area that I did not know and got hopelessly lost. I was looking for sign boards, street names, buildings that I recognized but couldn't see anything familiar. I phoned Steve in a panic and told him I was lost and his reply was "well, if you're lost how am I supposed to find you? Just walk east! And you will find your direction!"

I do not know my east from west, I battle with the concept of left and right and as I do not carry a compass the advice wasn't too helpful. But I did walk in the direction I thought was east and eventually came to recognize where I was.

When all had failed with my memory I had remembered "Go East!"

At 3am the phone rang, it was the hospital telling me that I needed to get there urgently. I did not question the urgency as I called a taxi while pulling on some clothes. I asked the taxi to get me to the hospital with speed which he did.

Once I arrived at the hospital I just saw the eyes of the night staff over the counter. They said nothing only pointed their fingers in the direction of Steve's room. They were terrified of going in and said only I could help him. I opened the door and saw the sight that had so frightened the nurses. Steve had got tangled up in the drips and fallen, so he had pulled them all out, there was blood gushing out of his arms where they had been. He was hallucinating and did not know who or where he was. He was so relieved to see me and hugged me hard in relief. He said he had been franticly searching for me as we had to get away as soon as possible because we were in danger. It was so hard to try and reassure him that everything was fine and he just needed to get back into bed. I could understand why the nurses were horrified as there Steve was demanding to be let out of the room, blood everywhere and the strangest thing ever, he had his fishing hat pulled tightly onto his head. It still evokes laughter each time we think about that terrifying sight and why on earth had he packed his fishing hat into his hospital bag? I think it might have been there from a previous trip we did.

Eventually I managed to calm Steve down and get him to sit on his bed. I wiped away the blood from his arms, removed his fishing hat and calm began to descend. I tried to ease him into bed but this was a mission and was only going to be accomplished by a mission. Steve agreed to get into bed provided I got him an ice cream. Steve rarely eats ice cream and never at 4am in the morning. So I rushed off to find an ice cream at 4am in the morning. I eventually found a 7/11 store and bought two ice-creams. Steve was so excited about the treat of an ice cream and we sat together on his bed eating them, after which he sweetly climbed into bed.

The doctor told the nurses to leave out the med drips and allow Steve a peaceful "night". He was tucked into bed arms free for the first time in days. While I had gone on "ice cream mission", the nurses had moved a day bed into Steve's room. They had made it up for me and told me that was where I was to sleep. The combination of cold turkey followed by a series of testing medication had an awful effect on Steve's system. It was incredible it should have been allowed.

Later that morning I was sitting on a chair outside of Steve's room having a much needed cup of coffee when the doctor arrived. He asked me "How is Steve's headache?"

I answered, "It's gone this morning but I have one now"

He replied "Me too." Cheeky!

The removal of all Steve's medication brought him back to where he had started the sweats, the pains and the unbearable headaches. He was determined to get through it with as little medication that he could. He began to do the pain with no medication. But there were just days when his body would not allow him to move and I had to call in the house doctor to give him Voltaren injections.

Steve was swimming to try and gain some of his physical strength back. He had been so badly coordinated and even holding my hand, he would still bump into things. For Christmas that year I had a bicycle custom made for Steve. He had loved his motor bikes when he was younger so I asked that his bike be made to look like a Harley Davidson motor bike. I ordered a bike for myself too, a Mary Poppins looking bike complete with little basket in front. I hid them in the basement car park and told Steve his Christmas present was in the post box. He humoured me and opened it and took out the key with a question upon his face. I pointed in the direction I had locked our bikes up. When Steve saw the bike he was overjoyed but also hesitant. He told me he had trouble walking, he did not think he would be able to ride a bike. I insisted that each day we practice in the car park and we did until eventually Steve one day said "let's go onto the road shall we?"

It was the beginning of our bike rides and we went further and further each day. A few months later I could no longer keep up with Steve and I would go half way and then turn for home while he ventured further. Things were improving. The tumour was still there as were the symptoms and it had not reduced through three radiation treatments but Steve was not about to give into it.

Steve

In theory when Dr Crazy explained what he wanted to do it sounded kind of logical, but in hindsight it was one of the most stupid things I have ever agreed to. Basically he was going to run cocktails of painkillers and sedatives through my veins, changing the types and mixtures every six hours, to see which combination eased the pain the most effectively.

In reality I ended up a total mental mess. One of the mixtures had me convinced Bev and I were being hunted by a group of people in a rather seedy part of some unknown city. It was unlike anything I had ever experienced and I was desperate to get us out of that situation. I had multiple-feed drips in both arms to enable the doctor to change the drug formulations easily without constantly changing the bags out for the next new mixture. During my efforts to get away from whoever was chasing us I needed to use the bathroom. Trying to climb out of bed with two drip stands on either side of a hospital bed whilst being on a mind bending drug induced trip is not the easiest thing in the world and within minutes of trying I was left lying on the floor of my room, tied up in the drip lines. I was vaguely aware of a nurse looking through the door at me, and all I heard was the door being closed and the patter of feet running down the corridor.

I was lying on the floor of my hospital room trying to figure out how to get the drip lines out of the main feeder line in my arms before "they" caught Bev and I. In the end I just grabbed the main drip feeder line and ripped it out of my left arm, and then did the same with my right. Free at last I hobbled into the washroom and wrapped toilet paper around my bleeding arms and went back and sat on my bed pondering my next move when the door opened and Bev walked in. The sight of her calmed me down immediately. I checked myself out of hospital the next morning.

There was one positive outcome of this horrendous experience with Dr. Crazy. I decided no more medicines. I could live with the pain, and with the aid of Xanax I found I could control the sweats to a large extent. I threw out every medication I was on – at one time I was taking forty eight tablets a day. Slowly I started to come alive again as the medications passed out of my body and I adjusted to not taking them anymore.

I had swum competitively for years at school and I started out using the swimming pool at our condo. I did a few lengths every night whilst trying to build up my strength and it was working. There was an amusing side to this though. I had very seldom seen anyone use the pool, but now as soon as I went to the pool at night there would suddenly be a whole bunch of other tenants who also wanted to swim. It was great. Especially moving for me was the sight of a young man in the block who was in a wheelchair with his legs amputated at his knees, who used to just sit on the verandah of his condo, day after day, just staring out. Suddenly one evening he wheeled himself out to the steps into the pool and after some time he managed to get into the water and started swimming – of a fashion. After that I would see him at the pool every day, and one could notice his progress as he got stronger and fitter and he started communicating with other residents in the pool.

Christmas came and Bev told me my present was in the post box. I through this was another of her pranks but humoured her anyway. I had a key in my hand and was wondering what was she up to now? She pointed across at the bike stand and I laid eyes upon my lovely red "Harley". It was fantastic, Bev had a local cycle shop make me bicycle that looked like a Harley-Davidson motorbike, but I did not know whether I could still ride a bike. We started practicing in the parking garage and eventually ended up venturing out onto the cycle paths alongside the canal. It was a great feeling. The bike was so unusual and eye-catching that other cyclists and pedestrians would stop and stare and comment on it. It gave me a lot of confidence as my balance and reaction time started improving straight away.

Chapter Eighteen

Happiness

Happiness is not something ready-made. It comes from your actions

— Dalai Lama

Beverly:

Steve needed a neurologist to direct his treatments as he refused to see either Dr Nasty and Dr Crazy. After much searching and visiting a variety of Doctors, neurosurgeon and professors, Steve finally settled for Dr Happy. Dr Happy was chosen because it was more convenient as he was at the hospital where Steve had started with all his treatments and he knew about the tumour having taken over the position of Dr HK.

Steve liked him because his visits there were always so positive. Dr Happy always had good news to impart. That is almost as bad as getting bad news all the time. After one of Steve's scans we went to see him. We had resigned ourselves to hearing the usual result that the tumour had not reduced and there was further growth. I was overjoyed when Dr Happy put up the scans and after turning them around to get different views of them, he announced that the tumour had shrunk. He traced his finger on a shadow like mass on the scan and then held up his pinkie finger, measuring just the top of it, he said the mass had reduced to a small size like that.

I couldn't wait to get home to tell everyone the news! Steve was just grinning from ear to ear. We felt like we had a massive reprieve. I phoned everyone I could with the news. I could not contain myself the next day I rushed off to the hospital where Steve had his adrenal gland and tumour removed and went to the suite of each of the three doctors who had been so part of this and told them the news. There was an air of celebration and joy. Dr R was ecstatic and rushed out to his reception area to tell his staff the good news.

Once it was all out and I no longer had anyone to tell, I got the feeling that something was not quite right. I went back into care giver mode and did my check list. Remember get a second opinion or a third. I read the scan report, it did not state anything about reduction in size in fact the measurements were larger. Scan measurements can be slight off course unless the scan is done by the same group all the time and not all Steve's scans were.

I went to my local GP Dr Wise with my concerns. Dr Wise had become a good friend. He was always relaxed and willing to listen to me. He calmed me whenever I was at a loss or overwhelmed. Of course I had run to his office too with the news of the magical shrinkage. I told him of my nagging feeling that something wasn't quite right. I explained that although Steve loved Dr Happy, I felt it was because he never put pressure on Steve. He did not do the *put your tongue out and follow my fingers with your eye test*. Dr Happy always had good news and a chat about current affairs and then gave Steve his meds so it was more like a social visit.

Dr Wise gave me the name of a Top Neurosurgeon who had been his teacher and arranged that I visit him. The Top Neuro was warm and wonderful; he listened and then looked at the scans. I had all the scans Steve had ever had with me. There were many and it weighed a ton yet I lugged them all in for comparison. My heart sunk and crashed as he told me that far from reduction there had been a growth. He called in a colleague who was a neurologist and agreed with his findings.

I was at a loss with what to do. Steve was so joyful; we had been elated at the shrinkage news. I had to decide whether or not to tell him. The doctor said that I was not allowed to withhold any medical information from Steve. It was a sad evening telling Steve that the tumour was still there.

As usual I think Steve knew all along, after all no symptoms had changed and there was no relief from the constant pain. He took it in a matter of fact way and although I was furious with Dr Happy, Steve was not. He still maintained that Dr Happy was only trying to make him feel happy and he had no ill feelings towards him. Steve had by this stage firmly said that he wanted no further radiation treatment, so he was quite happy to go along every few months for the checkups he needed in order to receive his medication.

I was so mad at Dr Happy and for a while my visits to collect Steve's medication were anything but "happy" for me as I tried to avoid him or if I did I shot him a wounded and disappointed look. He too developed an "attitude" towards me but slowly we were back to friendly terms and chats whenever I saw him.

Once again Steve and I found humour in the situation. We saw the funny side of my frenzied rush to tell everyone of the miracle cure causing such mass excitement but then having to return the following week and explain the mistake to everyone. I know the feeling of good fairy/bad fairy. As Steve's philosophy proved again, there was always someone worse off than you. Although I had felt so bad having to dash hopes once more, imagine the person who announced to his prayer group that it was their prayers that had miraculously healed Steve. We do have a warped sense of humour but that had us laughing at how he was going to explain that one!

It was during this time that I heard the news that Uncle Geoff, my Gran's husband had been brutal murdered in South Africa. This gentle, kind and loving man had arrived home after church and the attackers stabbed him. They left him in the back garden bleeding to death while they ransacked his home and piled his car with his belongings and drove off with it. The coroner said he would have slowly bled to death. I was upset, angry and battled to accept that a life could be so worthlessly taken. I felt heart broken and so sad.

Steve had a business trip to China. While he was away I was invited by Phil Merry and his wife, Normala to attend an international conference they were having in Singapore. Phil is a well-known motivational speaker, life coach and campaigner for happiness. It was called the First Asian New Science of happiness and well-being conference. I felt privileged to be invited and felt that once again, the universe had provided what I needed happiness and well-being. There were many international guests speaker, from a variety of the sectors, educationalist, doctors and motivational speakers all come together on the common ground of "happiness".

Phil had by chance seen the actress Goldie Hawn and shouted to her in passing "Would you like to attend a Happiness Conference in Singapore?"

To his surprise he received a Yes response. Unfortunately due to unforeseen circumstances she could not make it to the conference but sent her friend Dr. Judy Wallis on her behalf.

The conference was held at the Singapore Expo Center and the tables were packed. The speakers spoke about their own search for happiness, their experiences and the medical benefits of being happy. As they spoke happiness became contagious as it spread through the room.

Dr. Judy Willis took the stage. She was serenely beautiful and had a powerful quiet and composed aura about her. Judy is a neurologist, author, lecturer and educator, she radiated with happiness. She spoke about the brain and the effects of happiness. There was so much knowledge that she gave about the brain's activities that I wished I could to talk to her. Steve and I were constantly pursuing new avenues in an effort to understand how best to deal with the tumour. All through her talk I was thinking, "Wow what an amazing lady I really would love the opportunity to talk to her." But she was whisked off to an interview and other functions straight after her talk. The next speaker quickly replaced her empty spot and the conference continued.

Catherine Lim, a well know author from Singapore, gave a talk on happiness. She had us laughing until the tears ran down our faces she kept us spell bound with stories of her youth. She described "Once Upon a time Magic" and how it transcends natural lows and that imagination is the artist's greatest happiness. She was magic. I encourage you to buy one of her books and experience the joy, laughter and magic she is able to spread.

The conference renewed my energy and strength and I felt the power that happiness could give. Phil had also done an island wide search for Singapore's happiest people. The winner and finalist were there. They related their personal experiences on what it took to make them happy people.

I went home feeling more empowered than I had for a long time yet with that wistful regret that I had not meet Judy Wallis. Later that evening I received a call from Phil. He told me that Judy had such a busy schedule that she had asked for a quiet evening for the following night. He told me that he and Normala were taking her to Sentosa Island for a quiet dinner and asked if I would like to join them. I couldn't believe it. Of course I would love join them!

Phil mentioned that we would be going there by cable car. He knew that I had a fear of cable cars and heights. He suggested we met Judy at the lobby of her hotel then all proceed to the cable car station. If I felt I could not go by cable car then I could take a taxi from there and join them at Sentosa. It was all arranged and I just couldn't believe how lucky I was to be given the opportunity.

I knew that I could not bring Steve's tumour up in conversation that would be unthinkable and a "free consultation" from someone just wanting a nice quiet time out evening would be totally offensive. I was so impressed by Judy's positive attitude that just being in her company would be enough.

The night arrived I was feeling nervous. I thought at least with Phil and Normala present, I could be comfortable with just listening to the conversation. I arrived at the lobby with minutes to spare and then my phone rang. It was Normala to say that they were on the way but stuck in heavy traffic, it would be about another fifteen minutes before they got to the lobby. In the meantime could I please introduce myself to Judy and keep her occupied until they arrived. I had not expected that. I have always been reserved and prefer to be introduced rather than do the introduction personally. I gathered up all my courage and approached Judy as she entered the lobby. I explained that my name was Beverly and that I had been asked to accompany them to supper. Her warmth and spontaneous energy engulfed me. The fifteen minutes we waited flew by as we spoke about everything and I felt this was indeed a kindred spirit.

Phil and Normala arrived and we climbed into the car with them. As we headed towards the cable car station, Judy and I spoke nonstop all the way. When we arrived Phil turned to me and said "To go or not to go?"

I bravely announced that I would travel with them in the cab car to Sentosa. Phil bought the tickets and as we headed towards embarking he quietly whispered to me "Bev, I forgot to tell you, it's a glass bottomed cable car."

I gave a silent scream but too late now to back out. I headed toward the cable car with trepidation. I sat on the seat with Judy and Phil and Normala sat opposite us. One just could not fail to be under Judy's enthusiastic spell. I honestly did not have one nervous moment. Why I had I ever thought I feared cab cars?

It was long walk from the docking station to the restaurant but the beauty of Sentosa was all around. As we walked we were still talking and then in conversation Judy mentioned a rare kind of brain tumour. Before I even thought about it the words came out..."but my husband has that!" Judy was immediately interested and wanted to know all about it. When and how it had presented itself and what symptoms were currently being presented. We spoke about other topics with Phil and Normala at the table but she kept coming back to me asking for more information on Steve's tumour. It was an amazing night of shared HAPPINESS.

Once Judy returned to USA we wrote to each other. Both Judy and her husband were life savers for us, giving the advice and direction we so badly needed. I will forever be grateful for their generous and loving support of me at a time when I needed it so very badly. I would write Judy long mails about the daily happening in my life and she encouraged me to write a book about my moments for others to enjoy and reflect on.

CHAPTER NINETEEN

Celebrations - Steve turns fifty and new doors open.

It's only when we truly know and understand that we have a limited time on earth - and that we have no way of knowing when our time is up, we will then begin to live each day to the fullest, as if it was the only one we had.

- Elisabeth Kubler-Ross

Beverly:

It was almost time for Steve's fiftieth birthday. Steve had never thought he would make it to the grand old age of fifty. I wanted it to be a positive triumphant moment. So I set about making it really special. We had often spoken of going to the Hanging Gardens in Ubud but never quite made it due to the pressures and responsibilities that came with Steve's illness. In all our previous travelling Steve had always done the travel bookings, being a perfectionist he left nothing to chance.

I took matters into my own hands, booked a flight on an Asian airline and booked into the Hanging gardens Ubud.

I told Steve we were going away for his birthday and it was going to be a surprise destination. He asked if I knew what I was doing and I said of course!

So he jokingly replied, "Well, that's good but make sure we are travelling business class."

Oops! I phoned the flight center and upgraded to business the next day. I kept checking and re checking all bookings were in order and perfect.

I turned the focus onto the "surprise" holiday destination but what I was really doing was planning a surprise birthday party for Steve. I invited all those who had played a positive role in our lives. Like our wedding I wanted it to be a shared joy, a celebration that Steve had got this far, he had life! And it could only get better. Everyone accepted readily and so wanted to be part of the surprise.

I arranged it for a Friday night and organized for everyone to be there before Steve got home. Steve was still working for the local company and only arrived home at about seven in the evening. I had the party all set up and was waiting for the guests to arrive, when Steve called and said that the "boss" required him to work late. I begged Steve not to and please tell the" boss" that he could not work late. I told him that I could not be alone that evening. I needed him home. Steve was very puzzled as it was not like me to be so insistent that he come home. He was worried enough to get home a bit earlier and he walked straight into a chorus of "SURPRISE"! It was a wonderful fun filled evening of celebrating Steve's aliveness.

I was still doing double checks on our flight plans and hotel accommodation. All was well. The morning of our departure arrived. I called a taxi to take us to the airport. The taxi company prelists your addresses into the call center so they give you a few options that the taxi can be sent to. "Press One for ...." "Press Two for ..." I did not listen to the options just pressed for the Taxi to be sent to number one location.

We waited and waited, eventually I checked and I had sent the taxi to the wrong address. I had to redial and ask for another to be sent to our right location. Steve asked if he could know where we were going because he was a bit concerned about the holiday arrangements if I couldn't even get the taxi to the right address.

It was only when we were seated at the airport that I gave Steve the air tickets and destination. Steve groaned, I had without the knowing it chosen one of the worst airlines in Asia but at least it was business class. With a bumpy start to the flight and what can only be described as a hair raising kangaroo arrival we found ourselves in beautiful Bali. The hotel was stunning and we spent beautiful relaxed days in Ubud. We bought a painting there from a local artist of a baby yawning, our view of the world. It still has pride of place in our home.

Life was wonderful.

Something shifted and changed in Bali. We arrived home feeling more positive, renewed and ready to do battle once more. Steve was still feeling the full effects of the third bout of radiation treatments. Mostly, Steve fought the constant pain by swimming and going for long bike rides, trying to oust the pain by any means he could. More often than not though exercise only increased the pain and symptoms. Steve had always been motivated by sport and it was very frustrating for him.

Bev and Steve in Ubud – Steve still having problems trying to focus eye sight.

Steve:

I have never been a big one for birthday celebrations, which Bev knew, so I did not put two and two together when she kept calling me pressing me to come home early. I was still working with RL and we were in the middle of a large project, so I was working late every night. However, it was a Friday, so I decided to go home relatively early. What a great surprise. I opened the front door to be greeted by a handful of our closest friends, and a great night was had by all. I had never thought I would reach fifty so it was a bit of a double celebration for me.

There was more to come. Bev had a birthday trip planned. I was curious to see how she had done it and was most pleasantly surprised that she had even booked us in Business Class. However when I saw the airline I almost had second thoughts. At that time they had one of the worst safety records in the world and were banned from landing at most airports in Europe. Anyway, the flight was fine, apart from a rather bumpy "landing".

We stayed for a week at the Hanging Gardens in Ubud and it was great. It was wonderful lying in our private infinity pool looking out over the valley below. All too soon it was over, but it had given me a much needed rest and recuperation and I was feeling the best I had in a while. For now it was back to reality.

Beverly:

A short while after we arrived back in Singapore, Steve received an invitation to meet with a business connection.

E had often travelled to Singapore on business and would meet up with Steve whenever he could for some drinks and a trading of information about the industry. Steve had many connections and a vast amount of inside knowledge about the industry that he had gathered over the years. Steve has always been a mentor and nurturer of others. Every opportunity he ever had in life, he made sure that he has helped someone else along the way. He mentored many people and their careers and their loyalty to him remains strong. Steve went off for a few drinks with E not even thinking that this meeting could be any different to all the others. Steve arrived home with a grin from ear to ear. E had offered him a position in their company. They were setting up in Singapore and wanting Steve to set up for them.

Steve has always been an intellectual. He needs a great deal of mental stimulation and challenge to feel that he being productive. Steve's self-confidence had been seriously depleted through the years of living with the tumour. The treatments and all the other problems that came with them; the crippling financial costs, the lack of a "proper" job, the stress of just trying to survive both financially and physically, had hit him hard. I saw the light of enthusiasm, the excitement of the challenge and most of all hope shining through Steve's eyes that night. E would never know that he had thrown out a much needed life line to Steve.

Steve has never doubted his ability to work and give to the fullest of his devotion to his career. I had seen that when after each radiation treatment he would go straight to work and work a full day. A tribute to this amazing ability was the fact that people still consulted Steve with their business issues looking for the best advice and direction and looked to him for business development. No-one outside a very close circle knew that he was battling with a rare tumour. We were in no doubt that had people known Steve would never have been offered the positions that he was.

Steve:

I am unable to remember how E first made contact with me, but I think someone had given him my name and number in connection with some regional market information. E was the CEO of a company who was a market leader in their particular sector of the oil and gas industry. On his regular trips to his company's branch in Perth, Australia, he would stop off in Singapore to see a couple of clients and always gave me a call and asked me to meet him for a coffee and a chat. He would end up picking my brain about the region and any opportunities I may be aware of that could be of benefit for his company. I had no problem with this as he was a nice guy and we got on well and I was only too happy to share any information that might assist him.

We met regularly over the space of a year or so and he never touched on the subject of employment or making me an offer. During a major oil and gas exhibition in Singapore E called and asked if I could meet him at his hotel for a drink after the day's proceedings. I gave Bev a call and told her I was meeting E and would probably be home an hour or so later than normal.

When I got to E's hotel he was sitting with a group of people whom he introduced as the Chairman and Board members of his company. We had a few drinks and spoke about the region and my experience in it over the years. My mobile rang and I noticed it was a client calling so excused myself to take the call. When I returned to the table E asked me to have a look at something on the screen of his laptop. It was a job offer to become General Manager of their company in the SEA region and to set them up from scratch. The whole evening had actually been a confirmation of offer interview.

It was a very generous offer and would assist us greatly financially, so I accepted then and there. The salary was not the prime motivator in me accepting the position. All my life I have enjoyed building something from scratch and here was a wonderful opportunity given to me by E to do it again. Bev and I celebrated in fine fashion.

Years later E and I ended up as partners in our own international company.

CHAPTER TWENTY

The Hungry ghosts

The best and most beautiful things in the world cannot be seen or even touched - they must be felt with the heart.

- Helen Keller

Beverly:

Our financial situation was stabilizing and we could look at moving from our small apartment. We found a double story Terrance house. We loved the fact that it had its own gateway and a small patch of lawn in the front and back of the house. The move was scheduled for August.

The seventh lunar month in the traditional Chinese calendar is August and it is called the month of the Hungry Ghost. On the first day of August, which also happens to be my birthday; the Gates of Hell or the underworld are sprung open to allow ghosts and spirits access to the world of the living. The spirits spend the month visiting their families, feasting and looking for victims.

I had worriedly told the monks that the day the portals to hell are opened was in fact my birthday. I asked them if it was a bad day to have been born on. They reassured me that for me it was lucky but very bad for my poor mother as the birth would have driven her quite mad.

In order to appease these ghosts, ancestors are honored with offerings of food, incense, and ghost money - paper money which is burned so the spirits can use it. These offerings are done at makeshift altars set up on sidewalks.

As well as honoring your ancestors, offerings to ghosts without families must be made so that they will not cause you any harm. Ghost month is the most dangerous time of the year as malevolent spirits are on the look out to capture souls.

The month of the hungry ghost is a very inauspicious month. It's viewed as a bad time to do most things. Not a good time to open a new business or move to a new house, travel too is not a good idea. Most activities such as walking and swimming are frowned upon as there could be spirits out there wanting to do you harm.

The fifteenth day of the month is Hungry Ghost Festival, this is when the spirits energy is at its peak and they are looking to have a good time. It's important to give them a sumptuous feast on this day in order to bring good luck to the family for the rest of the year. Ceremonies are also performed on this day to ease the sufferings of the deceased.

Finally, the last day of the month arrives and this is when the Gates of Hell are closed up again. Chanting at the temples signal to the spirits that it's time to return and they are confined once again to the underworld; until the following year heralds a repeat of the hungry ghosts return.

Like most things I found about the hungry ghosts from Neena. When we signed our first annual lease for our apartment it was on the first of August. Therefore every year our lease was renewed on the first of August. We had no problem with this until I met Neena. We had decided not to renew our lease but to look for another home and we would be moving once our lease expired.

I was out to lunch with Neena when I explained that we had found another home and that I would be painting the interior of the old home before I moved out. I should have known from the silence as I talked that Neena was not happy with what I was saying. Once I had finished, she slowly shook her head and explained to me that it was the month of the hungry ghosts. Unsettled spirits walked among us and tried to cause mischief. We must always be on the alert as these ghosts were hungry and would consume anything they could. She told me it was not a good idea to paint walls during this period as I could inadvertently paint ghosts into the wall. Immediately I had an image inside my head of ghosts being splashed into the walls with my paint brush and then rolled into position with the roller. All in various postures of shock and surprise like cardboard cut outs, forever stuck behind a layer of paint. I suppressed a giggle as Neena was being very serious and reprimanding. She said it did not bode well that we were moving in the month of the hungry ghost as they were sure to take something from us in their hunger for revenge.

I did not let what Neena say worry me. I had lived long enough in Asia to experience all kinds of beliefs and customs. Besides I had moved apartment before in the month of the hungry ghost and all went well.

The day of our move was approaching and Steve and I went to look at our new home. We were so eager to move into this vast space after the confinements of our previous apartment. Singaporeans are always on the alert to save a couple of dollars. We had rented the apartment after two long negotiating conferences at the dining room table with the landlord, his wife and the estate agent. It was finally settled when the landlady's wife said she saw how much I loved her home and that she was certain that I would take good care of it.

They said they would move most of the furniture out but some would have to remain behind. This had happened in our previous apartment too. The landlord insisted on it being semi furnished in an effort for him to save on storage rental for the furniture he did not want to dispose of. That apartment did not have much room to start with and our furniture would not fit in with his. We offered to store his furniture so we could have more space for ours and the offer was readily and happily accepted.

The negotiations began again with the new home owners as to what would remain in the house and what would go. After managing to get a huge black vinyl couch, a horrific glass top dining room table and chairs removed, we had to settle for the fact that they were not going to move a long ornate wooden cupboard with a grey tomb stone looking marble top that took up the entire wall space.

Steve and I viewed our new home with approval but the sight of that cupboard was awful. We could not have it in our lounge and so we decided to store it in the maid's room. I thought that the furniture removals could move it out before they brought our furniture in but Steve was eager to remove it as soon as possible. He suggested that together we could move it into the maid's room. We each lifted a section of the cupboard. It was so heavy that as we lifted it the marble top section ripped from the wood and came crashing down on Steve's big toe.

We shifted the marble block aside and Steve's toe was crushed, it looked like a squashed banana and was a bloody mass of pulp. I wrapped it in paper towels and plastic shopping bags and then Steve drove in agony to the local clinic. Steve waited in the car, his toe bleeding profusely while I ran inside explaining it was an emergency and my husband's toe was crushed. They told me they could not help we would have to go to the emergency room at the hospital. Steve's face was white and I thought he would pass out but he calmly drove us back home. I called a taxi to take us to the hospital. We covered Steve's toe in paper towels and plastic packets so as not to drip blood all over the taxi. Once again a wonderful taxi driver drove us as fast as he could to the hospital.

The toe was a mess. The nurses were visibly affected by the sight of a toe so baldly squashed. The doctor said there had to be an emergency operation. I was feeling so nauseous and shaken up by all the blood and drama. Steve was the only one who remained calm. He looked at the doctor and said "Why all the fuss. No need for an operation. The toe has gone just cut it off!"

There was a shocked silence, and then the doctor's reply "Cannot Lah."

With that the preparation began to take Steve to the theater to stich up his toe.

Steve was not too happy with these developments. He has always been an avid Rugby fan and he had been waiting with great anticipation to watch an international match played by "his team" The Springboks. He told the doctor he needed the operation done as quick as possible so he could get home in time to watch the match. The doctor said it was not possible and that Steve would have to stay in overnight.

Steve asked if they had the TV channel on which the game would be shown they replied they did not whereby Steve said he would come back the next day.

I quietly drew the doctor aside and told him to humour Steve because after the anesthetic from the operation, he would properly sleep through till the next day. So the doctor returned to Steve saying he would see what he could do. The nurses removed Steve's watch, his glasses, mobile phone and wallet and told him that they would lock his valued possession in his room while he was in theater.

Steve was wheeled off to theater issuing dire threats if this operation should cause him to miss the Rugby. I settled back into the chair next to the bed in Steve's private room and let the quiet descend on me as I waited for Steve to come out of theater. After a while, I thought that it was perhaps a bit too quiet and maybe I should go and find a place where I could get a cup of much needed coffee. That is when I made the discovery that I had been locked in the room along with Steve's other valuable possessions. The door had been locked from the outside. All Steve's valued possessions were waiting for him when he was wheeled back into the room.

Far from being fast asleep Steve was very much wide awake. We had so many times during his treatments seen how mediation that would drop an elephant had little effect on him. This time Steve had refused to have general anesthetic and asked for local. He had also asked to watch while they operated as he wanted to see what they were doing to his toe.

The staff were more traumatized than what he was. His toe had been saved but the doctor informed me sadly that they had been unable to save the toe nail and it was unlikely that he would ever regrow one on that toe. Steve doesn't do unlikely well and within the year a nail has grown on the toe, a bit misshapen but a nail. I was just too happy that Steve had not had his toe amputated. It looked massive and very sore in its huge after op bandage.

Steve looked at me and said "ok let's go home now."

The doctor refused and told him to get into bed to recover and stay overnight. Steve lay on the bed for an hour constantly looking at his watch, and then he called the doctor and demanded to be released. The doctor refused and so Steve signed his own release form.

He arrived home with his hungry ghost munched toe with only a few minutes to spare before the Springboks played. To my great relief they won the match.

Steve:

The toe was mess, but once again I suffered no pain. The hospital clerk was taking so long with the admission paperwork that the plastic shopping bags over my foot filled up completely with blood which started overflowing onto the floor of the admissions room. A maid sitting with her elderly employer dashed over to try and clean up the blood on the floor under my wheelchair. I had to convince her that the hospital had their own cleaners' whose job that was.

My case came to the attention of the head of surgery who happened to be in the A & E room. He took a special interest in my case and decided to undertake the operation of sewing my toe back together himself. I really did not think they would be able to put it back together so told him to just cut it off as I did not really need it. The room went silent and everyone stared at me as if I was crazy. The doc told me that was not an option.

I lay on the operating table and the prof told me they would be giving me a general anesthetic prior to the operation. I firmly told him that was not an option and he should give me a local as I wanted to watch. There was just silence and dumbfounded stares. The Doc injected me with local in between all of my toes on my right foot and we waited for it to take effect. Whilst waiting two orderlies brought out a large strap and strapped me down to the operating table across my chest, and came back in minutes later with a large L-shaped piece of metal which they fitted in about two inches above my chest. I asked the nursing sister what these were for and she informed me they were for protection.

I asked, "Protection for whom?"

"All of us!" was her response.

The staff kindly set up a mirror and lights so I could watch the Doc operate on my toe. Once the operation started a kindly nursing sister stood next to me holding my right hand and stroking my arm. I was so interested in watching the op that I did not notice her stroking my arm at first but I eventually asked her what she was doing and she told me she was "comforting" me. I did not have the heart to tell her I was quite fine thank you and to go away.

After the op the fun and games began. The staff wheeled me back to my room and unlocked the door to a very relieved Bev, who had been locked in with my valuables. They started setting up a drip which they informed me they had to flush my system with antibiotics for twenty four hours. There was no way I was going to miss the Springbok rugby team in action. After much argument and signing off that I was discharging myself voluntarily and would have no claim against the hospital should there be any issues with the toe, Bev and I went home clutching a large packet of antibiotics.

We got home just in time for kick-off and my team won the game.

Beverly:

We were the only expats (expatriates) living on the road and both our neighbours were Chinese. The house on the right had their old grandmother living with them and she was very suspicious of us and always spying on us. She would break our plants, hitting at the palm leaves wildly with her walking stick as if she was confronting an enemy. She would move our dustbins and many other small irritations.

One day I confronted her and said, "No more choppie choppie. You choppie choppie my plants, I will choppie choppie yours!"

I pointed to her bonsai tree.

I showed her our plants she had ruined and after that we had a semi truce.

While living in the Terraced house we experienced our first Chinese death and its traditions. The Chinese are very family orientated, often there are three generations living in one household. Many have children because children are expected to look after their parents in their old age. They have a lot of tradition and beliefs based on their ancestors.

The Granny living in the house opposite our home died, immediately a huge marquee was set up at the cul de sac. It extended down the rest of the road covering the entrance to our drive way. A make shift temple was set up inside the marquee and flowers began to arrive. Hundreds of floral arrangements were put into the temple and all along the road. Bright colourful blankets arrived and were hung all along the fences of the houses in the neighborhood. As more and more arrived they were put onto the fences of the next road too. Tables and chairs were put out on the road along with a makeshift kitchen to feed all those who came to pay their respect. Many people arrived in huge groups and they lit incense and sung and chanted and did a viewing of Granny who was laying in state in the lounge. Bright lights were set up and they stayed on all the time. Each house that faced Granny's house, our house was the main one, had a huge red sticker stuck to the gate post. This was to keep the ghosts from entering our home.

On the first day, Steve and I were so excited to be part of the culture and to witness this magnificent sendoff first hand but after the third day it was enough of this depressing theme. Our lounge looked directly onto the activities and we could not move out of our gate due to the crowds. I was certain that even Granny would just like a bit of peace and quiet now to be able to continue her journey to the afterlife. I felt protected by the red sticker on our gate post because I am sure Granny would have preferred to float over to the quietness of our home compared to the frenzy activities, bright lights and viewing of her daily.

Day five started with crowds descending and first a group of ladies all dressed in green did a ritual dance along the road. A group of men with huge very happy face masks did a big happy dance to dance Granny happily into the other world. The monks played their instruments. Finally a glass cased

Hearst arrived. It had a massive photo of Granny pinned to the front of the vehicle and was covered in flowered wreaths. With much music and chanting Granny' coffin was placed in the vehicle. The monks walked in front playing their instruments and chanting. The Hearst slowly followed them and the huge crowd that had gathered followed the Hearst, Piped- Piper like to her final resting place. I think Granny must have been just as relieved as we were. The lights finally went out, the marquee was taken down, the road cleared of flowers, blankets, chairs and tables and the red sticker to protect us was taken down and in its place two mandarins and a two dollar note was placed as thanks for our patience and a sign of good will. Finally we returned to normality.

Our lives took on a routine living in our new home. Steve and I busy with our working lives and having long chats in the evenings about our daily happenings. Without the constant need for new medications, looking for solutions, radiation and scans, our lives had a feeling of normality to it. We still listened to advice from others and tried any solution that we thought might help Steve but it was not with the same frenzied hope for a quick cure.

One of the suggestions was that as Steve could not sleep he should have his sleep patterns checked. One night just about an hour before Steve was due to retire to bed; two "technicians" arrived sent by the Sleep doctor. They brought with them a machine and they fitted the wires from it onto Steve's head and chest with many plasters to keep them firmly in place. Steve patiently sat there while they rigged it all up. He waited until both technicians were in deep concentration over his head and he playfully yelled out at them. They got a terrible fright and Steve found it very funny. They said good night and they would return early next morning to collect the machine and the data it had stored on Steve's sleep pattern. Steve spent a very uncomfortable night attached to the machine.

The results the doctor found were that Steve suffered from sleep apnea. He was duly given a Continuous Positive Airflow Pressure (CPAP) machine to use a night. The CPAP device is a mask-like machine that provides a constant stream of air that keeps your breathing passages open while you sleep. A CPAP machine prevents sleep apnea by blowing air into a mask that covers the nose and mouth. The stream of air keeps the airways open. It was noisy and had Steve gasping as it strongly forced air down his throat. I lay awake because of the sound it made, it was way worse than occasional snoring; this was a constant whish sound. We both put up with it for about a week and then asked them to fetch the machine.

There were times I forgot all about the tumour. On one occasion Steve and I were doing shopping at our local supermarket. The center we went to had everything we needed. Dr Wise had his clinic there. Our hairdresser, optician, dry cleaners and Javanese massage parlor were all in the same building.

Steve was pushing the shopping trolley and I was putting in all the things I needed. Each time I asked him something he replied he could not hear me and I needed to talk louder. After a few minutes of this, I asked Steve to carry on shopping I would be back soon. I went to Dr Wise's receptionist and asked that Dr Wise syringe Steve's ears because they were surely very blocked. I hurried back into the supermarket and told Steve that I would continue to shop by myself as I had arrange for his ears to be syringed immediately. Steve took himself off. He walked in to see a very puzzled Dr Wise who asked what he could do for Steve. Steve replied that Bev had said he must syringe his ears. Dr Wise looked into Steve's ears and said they were fine they did not need to be syringed. Next time I saw Dr Wise I got a telling off from him. He had to remind me Steve had a brain tumour that would directly affect his hearing. Just for a while I had not thought of the tumour but had hoped for a natural solution to Steve's hearing problems.

There were times too when I would feel sad when I suffered from headaches, flu or body pains, because I knew medication would help and soon I would feel my normal self but these were the kind of pains Steve had to deal with daily knowing no medication could help.

Steve:

Dr. Wise is a wonderful man, who besides treating Bev and I for minor ailments, also provided an incredible amount of advice to Bev regarding my tumour and the side-effects it would produce. He and Bev became such good friends that if Bev was walking by his practice and noticed no patients in his waiting room, she would go in and have a social chat with him about various issues.

Bev and I were in the supermarket next to his practice one afternoon when Bev told me to wait and ran out the door. Bev came back after a few moments and told me to go in and have my ears syringed. I went into his practice and his receptionist told me to go straight into his consultancy room. I entered the room, shook his hand, and sat down. After exchanging a few pleasantries he asked what he could do for me today. I told him I thought he wanted to syringe my ears. He looked puzzled and I explained how Bev had told me she had arranged for him to syringe my ears.

Dr. Wise just burst out laughing. He actually had tears in his eyes. Eventually he took up his little instrument that doctors use to look in people's ears, had a look in mine, and told me my ears were nice and clean, and no, he was not going to syringe them. I could still hear him chuckling to himself when I walked out.

CHAPTER TWENTY ONE
Cambodia

My mission in life is not merely to survive, but to thrive; and to do so with some passion, some compassion, some humor, and some style.

- Maya Angelou

Beverly:

Steve had always loved business development and he was enthusiastic about hiring staff, setting up offices and doing exploration and development. He seemed to have great insight when hiring staff. He enjoyed giving people opportunities in which to develop their skills. He inspired and nurtured his staff. He changed lives. It was his way of giving back. I was so proud when Steve received a mail from an old colleague of his who had been diagnosed with a serious illness. He wrote that he had been in the most terrible pain and had thought of committing suicide several times. In those moments he would think back to Steve and how he had coped with his treatment and tremendous pain. He thanked Steve for being an inspiration to him, and by following Steve's example in dealing with the pain; he had saved his family from the hurt and trauma his suicide would have caused.

I was still working at Whatever, when I had the opportunity to travel to Cambodia and visit a shelter that rescued and protected young girls from human trafficking. I arrived to the chaos of Phnom Penh, the dusty air polluted roads and the hectically busy traffic. There were motorbikes everywhere, overloaded with stock, up to two dozen chicken strung together by their feet, huge bales of hay, enormous quantities of stuff that looked to tipple the bikes. There were whole families travelling together on one motor bike. Tuk tuks and huge trucks vying for a space on the road, traffic missing hitting each other by seconds. The people were so poor and destitute. Here it was not just street children but up to four generation families living on the streets. There were many victims of landmines which are still active in the area. Overcrowded, over noisy and over polluted. Yet the people I met where so kind and gentle.

I was to return to this place of Haunting beauty many times again on my own and work as international fund raiser for the shelter. But first I met the children, the beautiful children, who had been rescued from human trafficking. They had known such pain and suffering in their little lives. They were aged between five and eighteen and had all suffered the worst abuse imaginable. Some of the girls had been abducted from their homes, others sold by their own parents; each story horrifically horrible.

Most of the time I was given an interpreter to work with as I did not speak Khmer and the children did not speak English but I rarely had to use him. It's true that Love is a universal language and we could make ourselves understood.

One little girl Vee, was my inspiration. We connected from the first time we meet. She had the most amazing laughter I have ever heard. The joy of life and living just shone through her eyes and yet she had endured the worst abuse. I visited the shelter often and I would seek out her precious face and then she would be there running open armed to meet me and we would embrace. She was instrumental in changing my whole belief system. One day I watched as she quietly sat cross legged in a lotus like position in the corner of the room and quietly mouthed words of praise. She looked so beautiful, so content and so peaceful after all she had been through. Later when I spoke to the instructor she told me that it was the little girl's belief system that helped her and she was a Buddhist. I wanted some of her calm and acceptance.

I stayed at Frangipani Villa in Phnom Penh when I went there. It was run by staff who had previously been street children and were being trained in the hotel industry. I became a regular guest there and got to know the staff well, it was my home from home.

At the shelter I also helped the counselor set up the counselling department and helped with counselling some of the girls. I became friends with one of the teachers C, who gave me a lot of assistance into what the girls needed. I had always found dance to be therapeutic and healing and so each time I visited the shelter the girls and I would dance. I could see the healing effect it had on them.

I managed to set up a webpage www.rebuildconfidence. webs.com and through donations secured educational sponsorships; computers, playground equipment. My wonderfully generous husband Steve bought the girls a tuk tuk so that they would have transportation. They respectfully named it and put signage on it *"Steve's Tuk tuk"*. So if you're ever in Phnom Penh and happen to see a tuk tuk called *Steve's tuk tuk*, you will know the origin. When Steve heard that the house mother's husband died unexpectedly, he immediately sent her a generous monthly "salary" until she could get settled once more. He also paid all my travelling expenses and accommodation so that all the donations could go directly to the shelter; nothing was spent on "admin". It was Steve's way of giving back threefold.

Steve and I sponsored little Vee. Steve knew how I felt about her and had even at one stage said that we could "adopt" her. I did not think it would be fair to bring her out of her environment. The main objective was to reunite the children with their own families. Besides Steve and I were older and then there was the tumour. I had also learned a long while back when I was working with the bereaved children from my Hospice work that it was not good to get emotionally involved as a counsellor. It's your job to restore the children's confidence in themselves and their abilities and not become a replacement mother.

Helping those little girls healed me too. I loved my lone trips into the rural areas. I learned by doing things myself. I never felt fear or danger. The Villa that I lived in always provided my transport and kept a log of where I was going and what time I was due back.

Rebuildconfidence was also able to sponsor the education of five blind young adults for a year at another center in Phnom Penh. The center COMPED helps educate young blind people who had missed out on education. The teacher C, who had helped me so much at the shelter for the girls, had moved to the organization. The teacher became a dear friend and has been my invaluable connection in Cambodia.

The transport would vary depending on availability as the shelter was in a rural province way outside the town. The first time I went there by tuk-tuk was a terrifying experience. Most of the travelers have their nose and mouth covered with a cloth and I soon found out why. The dust was heavy and the fumes from all the vehicles toxic. I found myself heading to the shelter seated at the back seat of a tuk-tuk. I was surrounded by cases containing clothing and books, and big fluffy toys, donated by those who supported my efforts. So on the way there I was cushioned. Coming home it was another story it was just me and a vast open space. I felt every bump, every shift, every turn. We whizzed past huge massive trucks their wheels towering above the tuk-tuk, weaving in and out of traffic with breathtaking "just made it" moments! I hung onto the pole of the tuk-tuk for dear life, giving a whole new meaning to pole dancing.

Just when I thought I would never survive, humour came to the rescue. I noticed the back of my driver's t shirt it read COSMOS! I giggled at the sign that the universe was taking care of me.

On another visit, I was offered a local ride back which I gladly accepted. I was shown to a mini bus vehicle. I was placed at the very back seat, it was one seat but there were two other rows of seats in front of me. Being slightly claustrophobic, I reassured myself that once the two rows of seats had been placed back into position locking me into the small area of the back, I would be to move about a bit. Then they opened the hatch behind me and loaded it with all their goods to take to the market. Loads and loads till I thought they could fit no more. At the last push they stuffed in about thirty chickens all very much alive and all tied together by their feet. They were inches from my neck their glazed eyes staring directly at me. It took all my courage to stay sitting. Many people got into the vehicle and just when I let out a sigh of relief thinking there was room for no more, I was asked to shift up. A fellow passenger joined me in seat and my little space. Feeling just like those poor chickens, totally restricted in any movement, my long trip to town began. It had many stops and starts as they let people out and new ones in. I was so happy to see the Villa and receive the wave and cheery loud goodbye from my new friends.

I was travelling to the shelter with a young intern, Joe from the UK and two of the shelter's teachers. I was sitting on the seat directly behind the driver so I had my back to him. Joe was sitting opposite me, on the seat facing him. We were still in the city of Phnom Penh and we were going up a fairly steep hill when Joe shouted at me: "Bev JUMP!"

I looked at him bewildered, but he shouted again... "I really mean it JUMP NOW"

He grabbed my hand as he jumped pulling me off the vehicle with him as the scooter flipped backward, and the tuk tuk landed up in a nearby ditch.

We had to wait while it was pulled out and put back onto the road and then we were told we could get back on. I refused to get on before it had got to the top of the hill.

The poverty was awful and the people had nothing, on the way to the shelter we would pass through villages. Land mines are still a huge problem in the region and there were many victims of land mine explosions. There were beggars everywhere with lost limbs. The children were the most pitiful. The roads had terrible pot holes, worse when it rained as it was just slushy mud. Yet the moment we came close to the shelter my heart would sing at the stark beauty of the place. We would pass a large river that was filled with blooming pink lotus flowers and a huge ornamental story book looking Buddhist temple. There were always a few white cows walking around and grazing in that area and I knew that just around the corner the girls were waiting.

One day on the way to the shelter we passed by the local community who were gathered together to mourn the passing of a local person. They all joined together on the road. They had put massive drums on the road with food cooking away in them. The chairs and tables were placed in and across the road. I thought we would have to turn back and there would be no visit to the shelter that day but they happily invited us to join them in their feast. When we politely declined they help the driver of the car maneuver his way through the tables and huge drums of food bubbling and steaming away. I had visions of hot food flying everywhere if we hit one of the drums. The driver was skilled in avoiding the pitfalls and we were soon on the other side of the obstacle course and waved merrily on our way. Little did I know that a "party" like this one lasted for days and so it was the same maneuvering on the way back, accept this time there were more people to direct and shout instructions and cheer us on our way.

I was helping the counselor and we stayed in contact via email. I would send him information on counselling every week and give advice on some of the problems he faced. I was planning to return to decorate his counselling room with all the equipment he needed. Again my clients and friends generously provided when I asked for donations of equipment, toys, matting for the floor and books. It was such a shock and I was so sad that I ended up decorating the counselling room in memory of him. Just one week before I was to return Mr. S was killed. He was hit by a passing car while crossing the road. Mr. S was a kind gentleman, with a warm sense of humour and courage. He was totally committed to helping and healing the girls. His loss was tremendous. Once the supporters of rebuildconfidence heard the news, they collected a small sum of money which was given to his wife and young family he left behind.

I often wondered if one person could cause a shift or change and sometimes the work seemed dauting. I did try to create greater awareness and took a few different people to the shelter with me over the years to try and get greater coverage and support. Time and again, I felt sadly let down as on their return they would use their one visit as a publicity boost for themselves. Most of my guests never mention Rebuildconfidence and never went back to shelter again. Funds would be raised by others that never saw their way to the shelter. Others were just put off by the poverty, heat and what they perceived to be danger.

Whenever taking a guest with me I was required to get permission from the head of the organisation. If I had a guest, the director of the shelter would accompany us and pick up the guest from their hotels in the Organisations SUV so that there was minimal danger. They also asked that the location of the shelter be kept secret. This was for the safety and protection of the girls. While we were travelling to the shelter with the director, one of my guests phoned a friend and told the exact location we were going to. The director was most unhappy about this particularly as she had been asked not to reveal the destination, it was a direct breakdown of trust and I was told never to bring her back.

The shelter had barbed wire surrounding it, this was to keep "raiders" out. People who would want to Steal the girls away again. It gave it a shabby desolate prison like look. They had nothing but they had great pride and certain things were taboo. I always gave my guests a list of do's and don't while in Cambodia to read before they travelled with me but often these were not adhered to. My guests were also asked not to take photographs of the shelter or the girls which some of them did and used as publicity for their "involvement" in Cambodia. It was a breach of confidence and an invassion into the privacy of those young girls. I was so passionate and protective of those girls, that after a while and many let downs, I just decided that working on my own was the best way.

The shelter had nothing and yet they always gave. If I taught the girls a dance routine, they would thank me by teaching me a Cambodia dance, or teach me how to bow and greet in the Cambodian way. It was their way of giving back and saying thank you.

I had attended an angel workshop the week before my trip to Cambodia. I did not give out any personal information at the workshop and the lady giving the workshop was from Australia. She told me that I had green and pink energy around me and this was usually manifest around people who worked with children. She said that when Angels give out information like that it is always followed by a sign for confirmation. She told me that my sign would be that I would receive a gift in one week that was pink and green. I thought that would be impossible as I would be in Cambodia and unlikely to receive any gift there.

As I was leaving on my last day at the shelter, a young girl rushed up to me and hugged me and as she did so she pressed something into my hand. She showed me using signs that it was a gift for me from her heart. I opened my hand and to my astonishment there was a small ornament, a little white bear resting against a bright pink flower with green leaves. I tried to give it back to her but she was insistent that it was mine. It is one of my most treasured possessions. Some would call it a coincidence but I prefer to believe in Angels.

Many years previously I had reached a very low point in my life. I decided that I would no longer do counselling as it seemed so unfair to me that I seemed to be giving out so much hope and receiving very little myself. I decided to stop immediately I had four bookings for the following day. I called three and cancelled however I had no number to call and cancel for the fourth appointment so I resigned myself to doing this one last counselling session. I always took phone numbers along with the bookings and could not understand why I had not done so on this occasion. What was more intriguing is that the appointment was booked as Hercules.

The following day Hercules arrived; he was tall, has shoulder length fair hair and was dressed in white loose fitting longs and top. He was wearing sandals. He had a serene manner. He hardly uttered a word while I counselled him. He just sat there quietly taking all my words in. When I had finished and he was about to leave, he asked if he could hug me. As he did so he told me that he had travelled all over the world and had met many people but I had given him the most amazing counselling session he had ever had. He asked me to please promise him that I would never give up my counselling work. I was stunned as I had not mentioned anything about myself at all. I promised that I would keep on counselling and watched as he walked up the driveway into the bright sunlight. He had given me hope. Although I tried to find him, most of my work was done through word of mouth and contacts; no-one knew a Hercules. I was inspired enough to continue doing my counselling sessions. Years later I read that Hercules was the guardian angel of Leo's. I am a Leo; coincidence or an Angel?

I had learned to let go of fear and replace it with trust. Trust in myself and in the universe. By simply "going with the flow", I found that doors opened up easily and that there was always a connection to help me. Angels do exist in many guises and forms all you need to do in believe and they will manifest for you.

At the shelter I would be invited to join them for lunch. There would be a huge bowl of communal rice and a bowl of watery vegetable soup like broth. Each would have a smaller bowl and take small helpings at a time from the larger one. Much green tea was served during the meal. The dining area was outside under a zinc roof so terribly hot but all would gather at the wooden table and bench chairs and eat together. I felt privileged as I was made to feel part of their "family".

The first time I joined them for lunch, they cooked a fish with the vegetable broth, the whole fish with its head and tail. Throughout the meal they kept offering me the fish head because that is showing you an honour and respect as the fish head is thought to be the best part of the fish. The more I said "No thank you", they more insistent they were that I have it but the fish eyes were so visible. Eventually, as I could not speak Khmer and they had very little English, I explained with many actions that I was a vegetarian. They laughed and accepted that and afterwards I was only given vegetable dishes which was a relief.

I loved my years of working with the organization but sadly things began to change and corruption set in. Too many people, too many organizations were playing their role in Cambodia. It became a popular expat thing to be working for charity in Cambodia. Sadly rather than elevate the problems in Cambodia, this added to it as Orphanages were now seen as a lucrative business in Cambodia where children are the assets. The number of "orphanages" has increased sixty five percent in the past five years while in reality the actual number of orphans has decreased dramatically due to the recovery from genocide and AIDS epidemic. Over seventy percent of "orphans" living in these orphanages and shelters have parents but are portrayed as orphans in order to capitalize on the goodwill of organizations, volunteers and tourists. *see SISHA report.

When I first visited the shelter there were fifty eight young girls and a handful of teachers and staff. When I finally resigned there were five students and nineteen "teachers". While Joe was working there it was a good connection as together we worked well. Joe telling me of the greatest needs and then I would raise the funding for him. Unfortunately Joe left to take up a paying position with another organization and the cracks set in.

I was in Singapore and continued to send in sponsorship money for the girls' education. I would also send in funding when it was needed but I began to have an uneasy feeling. The more I gave, the more "problems" arose. I was told things like there was not enough money to buy the girls food at the end of the month yet most of their food was home grown. Joe had also set up chicken farming for them both for sale of eggs and for their own meals. He had also developed a large vegetable garden for them.

It was a worry that the financial demands became bigger and more demanding. We then found out that Steve was paying the house mother five times the normal monthly salary that was paid in Cambodia. Another "teacher" informed us we needed to pay her a salary too. Yet another teacher demanded a huge amount in US dollars for an operation for her sister, however she could not give details of the hospital or sister. I was beginning to feel like the shelter's ATM. I couldn't shake off the bad gut feeling so I planned a surprised trip to Cambodia.

I arrived at the shelter as the girls were getting back from school. I eagerly awaited the arrival of Vee. As the girls started appearing I wondered what could be wrong and there were too few girls. I confronted one of the "teachers". She told me that most of the girls had returned to their homes. Vee's parents had come looking for her and demanded she return home now that she was old enough to work in the home. The shelter had not told me about these developments. I was shocked and hurt, not only for myself but for my wonderful sponsors. The sponsorship money was still coming in regularly but the girls were no longer there and had not been there for a while. A few months previously, I had asked that the girls being sponsored please write a note to their sponsors. I had expected a little personal note from each one, instead I received twenty letters all exactly the same. It set off warning bells as in the past I had received beautiful personal and individually written mails with beautifully drawn pictures. It all fell into place now as the girls were no longer there.

With a heavy heart I resigned from the organization. Most of the young girls I had first met at the shelter had grown into young women in the seven years I had known them. Thanks to the teacher C, I met during my first years there; I still manage to stay in contact with Vee. I know how she is doing and if she ever needs help in life I will be there for her. For now she is doing well.

We learned that when doing voluntary work, it is not always a good idea to do monetary funding. This brings with it bigger problems and corruption. It's best to educate and empower. Work with the community in project building schemes. I loved my time in Cambodia but I felt it was now time for me to give something back to the country that had become my home and so I set out looking to see where I could be of assistance in Singapore.

It was amazing that every step of our way Steve and I had people step in and open doors for us when we most needed it. During my time of setting up www.rebuildconfidence. webs.com I received an email from Judy Westwater. It was another amazing coincidence that bought this "angel" into my life. Judy Westwater, is the author of Sunday times bestselling book "Street kid". She survived a tormented abusive childhood. She was forced to live as one of the street children in South Africa. She was determined to make her life meaningful and so she set up her charity The Pegasus Children's Trust. She works tirelessly to improve the lives of "street children" in violent South Africa and the rest of the world. In 2004 she was awarded a prestigious Unsung Hero's award for her amazing efforts. Judy was my inspiration and she helped guide me in all the right areas and gave me the encouragement I needed. www.streetkid.org.uk

Steve:

The challenges at the Shelter in Cambodia invigorated Bev and as usual, and she threw all of her energy into it. She was constantly busy, raising funds, accepting various gifts, emailing potential sponsors, most importantly, travelling up to the Shelter and taking an active part in counselling the girls, training the teachers and counsellors, and dancing. The pictures she took of the girls dancing show how much they enjoyed this activity – just huge grins and smiles.

I timed a business trip to Cambodia the first time Bev went to the Shelter; just to ensure she would be safe. I did not have to worry; they collected her from the hotel and brought her back safely in the evenings. Bev and I discussed as to whether or not I should accompany her to the shelter one day. I decided that this was not a good idea. These young girls had been sexually abused by adult men, both local and foreign, and I thought my presence would not be good idea. Although I never physically went to the Shelter with Bev I had the pleasure of seeing her amazing work through the photographs she took.

Even though we were not exactly flush with money ourselves we contributed financially whenever we could. However, once we started this I noticed that the demands become more often and always for ever-increasing amounts. I started getting a bit wary when Bev would show me photos of one of the teachers at the Shelters home on Facebook. In the back-ground we could notice many of the toys and items Bev had taken to the counselling room at the Shelter. Seems this teacher thought they should rather be at her home for her children.

The demands for money were increasing by the week and one day one of the teachers called Bev and started demanding money as they had no food at the Shelter. This particular day we noticed on the home page of the head of the Shelter that she was once again in some fancy hotel in another part of the world, attending yet another conference. This was becoming a regular thing and the photos of all of the places she was visiting started piling up, whilst at the Shelter we were receiving continuous calls for more money.

Bev and I had a discussion about this and decided no more money. She would continue to assist but only with educational assistance and project building schemes. The pleas for more money soon trickled off to nothing. I was sad for Bev as she had taken such pride in what she had done at the shelter and here it was being ruined by rampant corruption and lies.

CHAPTER TWENTY TWO
Travels and Monks.

Wherever you go, go with all your heart.

- Confucius

Beverly:

Around this time Steve was hectic with travel and setting up the new company. We had a major setback though when Steve went for his scan result after the third bout of treatments. We were told there had been no reduction, in fact growth was indicated. It was a moment that we both realized that there was no solution for this tumour, it could not be cut out, it could not be zapped away with radiation. It was still there! Steve decided then that he would have no more radiation treatment and stop our huge search into "Cures". Steve had experienced it all and survived; in the words of Frank Sinatra Steve simply... "Did it MY way!"- Steve's own instinctive way.

The thing that hurt the most was that some people who knew about the tumuor didn't think it was that bad. If it had been outside growing where people could have seen the ugly uncontrollable mass he would have been afforded more sympathy. But we got the feeling that with most people it was "out of sight out of mind". This horrid mass was growing inside where no-one could see it. Often comment such as "Oh its only Benign tumour and not cancerous" did not help either. Steve looked so well and so there was no support system for either of us but we had each other.

Steve also did extensive travel throughout Asia for his firm. Often I would accompany him and go on my own little adventures while he did his business meetings. The firm put us up in five star accommodation which is truly wonderful and top luxury in Asia. Steve needed to do a business trip to Bangkok and I decided I would go with him. When we arrived our luxury taxi pulled up alongside the limosines in arrival area. The staff opening the car door for us and welcoming us to their resort. Elegance and class.

Steve left early in the morning for his business meetings so I decided I would walk to a huge well known shopping complex that was frequented by all the toursists. In the lobby the hotel staff immediately went to call one of their luxurious vehicles to take me to my destination. I told them not to and asked how long it would be to walk to the complex I wanted to go to. They said it would be better for me to be taken there by car. I informed them I felt like the walk. They said it would take me about twenty minutes to walk there.

Bangkok traffic is horrendous and a twenty minute trip could take over two hours or longer due to heavy traffic congestion. Bangkok is pedestrain friendly they have elevated pedestrian walkways that are above the roads, they are called sky walks. They have cover and they have steps leading off at every few blocks. So I set out along the sky walk. I walked and walked and I had still not reached the shopping complex. I stopped someone and asked how far it was until I reached the complex.

He said, "Ten minutes."

I walked for ten minutes and stopped the next person and asked "how long to the complex?"

She replied, "Ten minutes."

After I had walked another ten minutes and asked a third person, "how long?"

They too replied, "Ten minutes"

I realised that ten minutes must be the given answer to everything.

I walked down the exit steps and onto the bustling congested sidewalk of the road below. Immediately I got shouted at and beckoned from all corners by hawkers begging me to buy their road side ware.

I pushed my way through the masses until I saw an elegant local lady standing on the sidewalk. I approached her and asked if I was anywhere near the complex.

She told me, "You are a ten minute walk away".

I laughly told her everyone had told me ten minutes and I had been walking for almost an hour.

She replied, "No matter, it is too early and the complex is not open yet. It will only open in two hours time but you like jewellery? You must see the factory shop where street children have been educated into making jewellery."

Before I could say a word, she was on the edge of the pavement and wildly flagging down a tuk tuk. Eventually one pulled across three lanes of traffic, I thought he would be hit by the huge trucks as he manovered his way around them. It was the oldest looking tuk tuk I had ever seen. The seats and roof cover were torn, dirty and tatty. The vehicle had rust holes clearly visable. The lady shouted to him to be heard above the noise of the traffic. She told him that I would pay him twenty US dollars to take me to the factory, then the complex and then back to my hotel. He must wait for me at all places and make sure no harm came to me and he promised to do so. I still had not uttered one word. She then took me by my arm and pushed me into the tuk tuk telling me it had all been taken care of and I was not to pay the tuk tuk driver until he had delivered me safely back to the hotel at the end of my day. The tuk tuk pulled off a neck breaking speed into the heavy polluted traffic. I was terrified at the weaving we were doing around the traffic. Down alleys, over pavements and I hung on for dear life as the tuk tuk rattled and shook. I had no idea where I was or where I was being taken. After what seemed like a very long trip, the driver slowed down and pulled into a parking area. There were many tuk tuks parked there and he pointed in the direction of a large building and indicated he would wait for me.

I was welcomed at the door and lead into the "factory". I was shown a bit of history about the place. They had taken in street children and were giving them life skills and training them to be jewellers. Once I had heard the story of the orgins of the "factory", they opened the door for me to enter the work section. I felt I had entered Aladdins cave, in every spare space there were huge woven baskets filled with every kind of semi precious stone. I walked about as the workers were busy designing and making the jewelery. After the heavy traffic and noise from the outside it was wonderful to be in a calm, quiet environment. It was amazing to see people so happy at being creative and everyone gave a warm and genuine greeting to me as I passed.

Once I had seen the work shop I was lead into the sales room. There was counter upon counter of beautiful stunning jewellery. I wanted it all. I spent ages looking and admiring until I found a few beautiful pieces that I bought. I had spent almost two hours in the "factory". It had been a wonderful experience.

I said a cheery goodbye and step out into the bright sunlight and noise once more. I suddenly felt nervous as I could not see my tuk tuk driver. There was row upon row of tuk tuks and they all looked the same. I stood there not knowing what to do and hoping that the driver would spot me. I felt sure he would as I had not paid him yet. It was so hot and no driver came in search of me. After what seemed a long while, the lady who had shown me around the factory came outside to join me. She told me it was not safe to stand where I was and I explained to her about my tuk tuk driver.

She briskly said "Come with me."

I followed her and as we passed each tuk tuk, she would turn to me and ask, "Is that your driver?"

Each time I said no and we continued the search in this way. Then, we came to a rusty grubby tuk tuk parked in a shaded area, the driver was asleep on the back seat. Hands on her hips, she called me to take a look. "Is that him?"

I answered that it was. Before I could do anything, she reached into the tuk tuk, pulled him out by his shirt and slapped him across his face a few times. She shouted loudly "You are being paid to be this woman's protector and you are not doing a very good job! You will now take her to the complex, you will remain awake and alert and wait for her and then you WILL deliver her to the door steps of her hotel."

She then screamed further abuse at him then she turned to me and apologised for him. She helped me onto the seat where the driver had been so soundly asleep a few moments before. I was speechless. The driver reved up and we jerkly pulled off into the heavy traffic again. I closed my eyes not wanting to see the dangerous manouveors through the traffic.

I arrived at the complex feeling shaken and I no longer felt like shopping. Walked around the massive complex I felt claustrophobic by the crowd all pushing their way through and the noisy shouts and chatter wore me down. After a few token purchases I returned to the tuk tuk driver who was waiting wide awake and alert and ready to perform his next mission to see me safely to the hotel. It was a relief to see the familiar surroundings that indicated we were close to the hotel. When we were about a block from the hotel, I shouted above the noise to the tuk tuk driver that he could pull over and I would walk the rest of the way. He was very firm in his reply, he had promised to protect and deliver me safely to the hotel doors.

The entrance to the hotel was in from the road and in a curved shape, ahead of the tuk tuk were two luxury vehicles and a limo. The staff opened the vehicle doors and with genteel manners greeted them. The tuk tuk made a noisy, back firing, smoke polluted pull up behind them. The staff came down the stairs to greet me and paused not sure of the etiquette involved when welcoming a wind blown, shaken up guest from such a dirty and falling apart mode of transport. I tried to remain looking like I had it all in my stride as I handed the driver his twenty US dollars and he speed off noisily. As I entered the hotel the staff asked politely, "Had a good day Madam?"

In my best voice I replied; "Yes, thank you".

Steve and I would always meet for a pre dinner drinks on his business trips and he had quickly learnt that when he asked "how was your day?" that my answer would involve a very long story.

Our Terrance house was near a huge Buddhist Temple and I would visit there and just absorb the peace, calmness and acceptance. The monks noticed that I was visiting often and so they started to give me instruction. Again, there was a language problem but we got to understand each other perfectly. They were gentle in their guidance and became my friends. I would regularly go to the temple, remove my shoes at the bottom of the steps and quietly join the group of chanters. The nuns would guide my fingers over the Chinese letters, starting from the back of the book and moving my finger along the column starting at the bottom right-hand of the page and moving upwards. I gently touched each Chinese letter with my finger as I learnt to hum along. Many days I would sit with the mediation group and under the guidance of visiting Tibetan monks we would chant the OM MANI PEI ME HON mantra over and over. It brought such calmness to my soul.

Often, in moments of despair and uncertainty, I would enter the temple and sit in that still quiet place on my own. I could allow the tears to flow and I would leave feeling a sense of calmness and peace. I would light candles and incense and beseech the Buddha of Medicine to help Steve; reciting the mantra "NAN MO YAO SHI LIU LI GUANG RU LAI." I would try to get to the temple by midday as this is when the monks would play their various instruments and chant. I called them my "boy band"

I was visiting the temple when one of the monks indicated that I should follow her. She took me through to one of the inner temples where she and another monk made a prayer bead bracelet for me. They blessed each bead as they put it together and once it was finished they lovingly placed it on my arm and called me sister. They also gave me a beautiful bead necklace, both the bracelet and the necklace are used much like the rosary to count each mantra as it is said. The necklace was given to me after the monk asked how many times I had recited my mantra. I indicated the beads on my bracket. The monk shook her head and showed me that I needed to do it more times than the beads on my bracelet. She handed me a very long beaded necklace with which to do my future counting.

How sad though that the modern world seems to have crept in everywhere. I so loved the ancient rituals so I was more than a little shocked when I attended a mantra session of a visiting Lama. He sat on a large chair evaluated above us sitting on the floor. The monks surrounded him with their drums and boom, boom, boom; the rhythm was being set for the mantra. Then one of the monks came around carrying a box and from it handed each of us a plastic ring to put on our pointer finger. I did not know what to do with this object until the lady sitting next to me showed me to switch it on as it was a digital counter. They were all very excited at this new method of keeping count on the mantras. I way preferred my bead count!

The monks also gave us a big marble statue of Buddha which has pride of place at our front door. In all of Asia I have only been given so much by those who have so little to give, not only material things but huge life changing and shifting values.

I arrived at the Temple one morning and the monk was eagerly awaiting me. They took me over to the adjoining temple and with joy it was announced they had found someone who could talk English. They introduced me to a serenely beautiful lady. She had that same tranquil qualities that I had seen in little Vee from Cambodia, it radiated from her. I introduced myself as Beverly and held out my hand to her and she replied "Why."

Her reply had me totally puzzled as to how to answer. Was she asking why was I Beverly or Why What? As nothing could come to mind quickly enough I just said "And what is your name?"

Again she replied "Why".

It was only then I realized that her name was in fact Why.

I learned so much from her, she became my mentor in all things Buddhist. She would often invite me to the functions and I would feel blessed to be part of this Tibetan culture. One evening Why invited me to the ceremony of "One bow three steps"

She explained this was to give thanks for all we have in life and so everyone would walk a circular route around the temple for an hour. The Participants would form in a long line and proceed to walk in the format of three steps and then one bow. The dress code was a black pajama like suit. They told me the temple had plenty of them so I could use one. It brought a round of laughter, when I showed how I towered above them all and the long top would barely cover my bottom. They laughingly agreed I could wear my own assemble of black longs and top.

I arrived at the temple to take part. I stood back to observe before I joined the Congo like line weaving its way across the temple. I was so thankful I did because I could never have done the steps. I had imagined that one bow was just a bending at the waist and leaning a bit forward but this bow was not like that. It was slowly melting down the knees and then full out prostrate onto the ground. Then getting up gracefully and doing three steps and the bow all over again.

It was done with such reverend poise and elegance. I could imagine how my bow as I got up would act as a domino trigger and have everyone else falling backwards too. So I had to decline any participation but it was a magnificent sight to see.

I was also asked to join the choir. I went along to one practice evening but it was all in Chinese. All I could do was try to hum along but even then the music took on variations I could never hope to follow. I had to beg off participation there. I did contribute to the temple by writing a caregivers manual that they could use to train others.

It was so different to anything Buddhist I had ever experienced. It is not a religion it is truly a way of life. They never talk about their belief system to others and are totally accepting of other peoples choices not matter what their religion or culture. They believe that a true Buddhist shows the light to others by just BEING. I had experienced that from both Vee and Why. No matter what life had thrown their way, they were beautiful, serene, calm and accepting. Just that one word Acceptance, helped overcome so many fears.

I was embracing the word ACCEPTANCE.

Steve too had slowly reached the level of Acceptance. He reached a point where he knew that the tumour was not shrinking and that he would have to adapt his life to the symptoms as they presented themselves. He did not want any further radiation. He accepted that all he could do was to have regular scans to monitor the growth of the tumour. Steve accepted that pain was part of his daily life. With Acceptance we had come so far from the frantic desperate searches for complete recovering, all the doctors, the medication, the seeking. The tumour was there, it had not responded to treatment and it was growing but Steve had not let it win the battle.

Steve:

With Acceptance came peace. I no longer worried about the tumour. I was used to the constant pain and learned to adapt to it. When one lives with a constant severe headache one eventually becomes used to it, as with the bodily pains. I decided that regardless of the results of the scans I would have no further radiation treatments. I just wanted to be aware of whether it was growing or not.

I was also unsure as to whether I could undergo another bout of radiation due to the build-up of scar tissue around the tumour from the previous treatments that the doctor had told me about. So that was it. No more.

Chapter Twenty Three
Melt down and finally Acceptance.

"With everything that has happened to you, you can either feel sorry for yourself or treat what has happened as a gift. Everything is either an opportunity to grow or an obstacle to keep you from growing. You get to choose.

- Wayne W Dyer.

Beverly:

I decided to move into self-employment and found a lovely serviced office in the business center of Singapore at U E Square. It was very business-like and professional and my client base that was seeking counselling were mostly professional business people. I enjoyed my busy days there and the environment felt very comfortable. I enjoyed interacting with people and advising. I made many contacts who generously gave to the causes www.Rebuildconfidence.webs.com supported. I no longer had long walks or waits to find transport home as I walked straight from my office to a waiting taxi each afternoon.

Steve's work involved a lot of travel and at every opportunity I travelled with him as well as traveling to Cambodia. Yet soon I found myself suffering from deep depression. My work was isolating me. In all my other positions there was a "family element" shared joy and laughter between breaks in seeing clients. U E Square had a large number of serviced offices all rented by professional business companies. Aside from the "good morning" to the receptionists and to other business people I passed in the corridors or at the coffee machine there was little interaction with others. My clients would pour out their hearts to me about their most intimate problems and would be so happy and grateful for the advice I was giving. Little did they know that the minute they left I would go to the washroom and cry, I just could not stop the tears from flowing. I would apply fresh make up and be ready to greet my next client with a smile and some advice and guidance. At the end of the day I would cry and cry in privacy of the washroom before making my way home.

I realized that I was suffering from melt down, all the years of being strong, and holding everything together had taken its toll. I mourned for the loss of me. My strength and humour had ebbed away. The tumour had eaten away at so much of our life together. I had held everything deep inside me telling myself and believing that I was strong and I could cope. Even the strongest of us needs a support system. I felt alone and isolated. Steve was struggling on a daily basis and I could not add to his pain but I felt that tumour invade my soul as it was invading Steve's head. I had forgotten how to smile.

I had a sense of dread and apprehension. The news arrived that my ex-husband had been diagnosed with stage four colon and liver cancer. I was not in a good place to cope with the news. My sons were devastated. They took loving care of their father along with their aunt Georgie. I was not coping emotionally. I cried all the time. Some evenings I would sit outside and weed our small patch of lawn and hear the pitiful mournful songs sung by the maid next door. I could hear her sadness and longings and I would weep along to her songs. I just felt life was so unfair and cruel.

I was not feeling well physically, I felt ill and drained. I woke up one morning with the dreaded feeling that I needed to go back to South Africa as soon as I could. I never questioned the feeling, although my sons were living on hope and firmly believed that their father would recover. It was hard for me to put all these feelings to Steve but he insisted that I go at once and made all the arrangements. I was in awe of his generosity of spirit and his insistence that I needed to be there. I knew it was not easy for him.

I arrived in South Africa and my youngest son collected me from the airport. I was so shocked and saddened to see his father. I knew that there was very little time left and called my other two sons to come home. His sister Georgie arrived to stay with us and help feed the constant flow of visitors. I switched off emotionally and took over the task of nursing him. It was hard to see him in such physical pain and he could no longer communicate. The emotional pain of my children tore into my heart. He passed away six days later, peacefully surrounded by the family he loved. I will be forever grateful we got the chance to say goodbye.

Flying home I felt violently ill. I kept telling myself it was the effects of the mourning and emotional trauma. It was so fortunate that my seat on the plane had two empty seats next to it and I spread out but I was in agony. I couldn't eat or drink anything. I had a stopover in Dubai and as soon as I was off the plane I spent most of the connection time being ill in the washroom. I got onto the connecting flight feeling drained and shaken. I have never felt so relieved to arrive in Singapore.

Steve put me to bed, also thinking that it was stress and exhaustion. Two days later, I suffered a huge painful attack. I called Steve and he rushed home from work. He was horrified to see the pain I was in. He rushed me to the nearest hospital where I was immediately admitted. We had often heard the locals comment about this hospital; "Once in – never out!"

We had wondered why they said that. We were about to find out.

It was a "teaching hospital". The doctors arrived with an anchorage of interns who stood around the bed discussing what could be wrong with me. I was in agony, the pain totally unbearable. I was put onto drips and morphine. I was taken to have scans done. The results came back that I was seriously dehydrated and had chronic pancreatitis and gall stones. They say they needed to operate immediately. I sobbed that I was just too ill and exhausted to even think about having an operation at that point and they just needed to get me well first.

It was a dreadful experience. I was sick, I was sad, I was in agony and yet they continued to surround my bed each day and prod and poke away at me as the interns decided on a diagnosis. I was kept in hospital for ten days on a drip and no food allowed. I was so hungry that I begged one of the nurses for a chicken stock cube in a bit of water. She kindly sneaked it to me and I have never tasted anything so good. The doctors said I would not be allowed home until I ate but they weren't feeding me. I was so weak and shaking all the time. I could barely walk to the bathroom and I begged for a bath. I was taken into a big open room and sat on a chair while the nurses hosed me down.

Each day I would be taken off for yet another scan just to make certain and be re diagnosed. One evening after 10pm a group of interns entered the room saying I was about to go for yet another scan. I shouted "no more enough!"

I phoned Steve in tears and the next morning he was there to take me home. We had to sign documents to say that I was releasing myself. We got to know why the locals said "once in – never out."

Needless to say with all the scans and tests, the medical bill was enormous but once again Steve's kind banking system helped us.

I was home for just two days before the pain hit me again. Steve rushed me to the catholic hospital that had been so wonderful to us despite his "fishing hat episode". The doctor there said I needed to have my gall bladder removed immediately. I had it done the following morning. It was the first time I had an operation where I woke up feeling so much better. The relief was tremendous. I only spent one night in hospital following my operation as I left the doctor handed me a jar of big hard misshapen stones that had formed inside my removed gall bladder.

In the calmness of my bedroom and slowly recovering I took a good look at those hard awful stones and realize that this was what disease looked like. I had been at Dis Ease with the tumour. The tumour had its full effect on me, everything I had internalized had in turn manifest into these harsh stones. As soon as I was well enough I took a taxi back to where I had originally found healing and that was the East Coast.

I walked out onto the jetty, the breeze gently blowing through my hair and I felt calm and at peace. I had no more tears, no more a feeling of depression rather a sense of elation as I knew that Steve and I had proved to be survivors. Together we could overcome any obstacle and each obstacle had only strengthened to bind our love more strongly. I gave silent thanks to the universe for the great adventure it had bestowed on Steve and me. I knew that we would have the rest of our lives together. I held the stones above my head and threw them as far as I could into the sea. I was whole again.

Together Steve and I had walked through the five stages of grief associated with his illness.

Denial and isolation:
Anger:
Bargaining:
Depression:
It felt so good to have finally arrived at the final level **Acceptance**.

In many Shamanic societies, if you came to a medicine person complaining of being disheartened, dispirited, or depressed, they would ask you four questions. When did you stop dancing? When did you stop singing? When did you stop being enchanted by stories? When did you stop finding comfort in the sweet territory of silence?

Steve and I decided that I had put too much energy into the lives of others and not enough into nurturing myself. So I no longer did full time counselling and began to explore the beautiful city of Singapore once more. One day a week was my day where I would look for a new place to visit, I did not invite anyone to join me as I loved the solitude. I have never been a house wife or ex pat functions material and so I began looking for something to fill my days. Steve asked what I would like to do and I said study dance again. I saw the joy and healing effect it had on the girls in Cambodia and I wanted to be able to professionally heal others through the medium of dance therapy.

I enjoyed my studies immensely and as I studied new doors began to open for me. Doctors and education departments had seen the benefits of dance therapy and I began working with them to improve the lives of young children and adults. The physical and emotional aspects of dance bought healing to my soul too. I now teach dance movement therapy and am international recognized in my field of dance. It's the most incredible feeling to see the joy of dance.

A young student who was locked away in her own world with autistic like characteristics, came alive to the sound of music and took up the entire room as she entwined herself into and became the music, it was a dance of pure JOY.

Students with low self-esteem and confidence grow and blossom as dance flows through them and for a while all their troubles, worries and problems are forgotten as the music takes over and they are transported to another sphere.

New exciting doors in business opened up for Steve. He is internationally recognized in his field of work and is beginning to reap the rewards. He was offered a partnership and their firm is developing and spreading worldwide.

With Steve's new position he felt more secure than he had in years and it enabled us to find a home to make ours. Again it was by chance that we saw a vacant house. It was everything we both wanted. It had a large garden with a swimming pool, a rare find in Singapore. Steve loved the swimming pool. When the pain becomes too much, he no longer needs to lie in a dark room and imagine he is swimming to his special island. When he needs peace and solitude and an escape from the pain he goes swimming in his pool. It is the most therapeutic source of healing for him.

Opposite our house is a Buddhist temple. Its sacred ethereal energy flows directly into our home. We float in the swimming pool to the sound of devotional chanting emanating from it. The peaceful rhythm and chatting reminds us to remain connected to our inner source of acceptance.

Steve:

The new house was a wonderful find. What appealed most to me was the large swimming-pool. Water – my magic potion. We sit outside in the evenings as dusk is falling and listen to the chanting coming from the Buddhist temple opposite us, as the birds settling down for the night in the large trees behind the house.

We love watching the activity at the temple. We can view the monks sitting in their rooms with Tibetan curtains adoring their doorways, watch their ceremonies and just feel contentment as their peace washed over us. We laugh at the thought that if we could see them then surely they could see us.

I am an avid sports fan and always watch games of rugby or soccer on Saturday nights. One particularly hot night after watching a rugby game Bev said "Let's have a midnight skinny dip", so off we went. No sooner had we stripped off and were relaxing in the pool than a train on the MRT behind the house came to a stop parallel with the pool. All the lights in the train were on and we could see people sitting and standing in the train. Bizarre we thought. This was most unusual, had the train stopped due to some line instruction, or was the driver just perving at us?

We'd recently been through the longest drought in Singapore in the past fifty plus years. The grass was brown and even some of the toughest shrubs and trees started dying. I had the water sprinkler going every day. The heat was relentless. Then one evening we heard the thunder, followed by a heavy downfall that just went on and on. It was as though a breakthrough of some kind occurred in me as well and at the same time Bev. We jumped up and went outside and danced together in the pouring rain on our front lawn.

Life had not given give us the path we had planned together but it was not good to think of "what ifs".....what if we had met when we were younger, what if the tumour hadn't dominated our lives? We had taken on more than most people experience in a lifetime and we had done it together. Without Bev in my life I don't think I would have survived. Life had woven our paths together and it had been worth waiting for. Together we had arrived home. I realized that whatever life would throw at us, our love would carry us through.

Beverly:

I really think that there is something out there and when it is our time to go, we are not judged by what others gave us or how they treated us but by what we achieved and what we did for others and maybe also ourselves. You don't have to be religious but you do need to have a belief system. We truly believe in the Buddhist principle that we are simply where we are meant to be every second of every day. The best way we have managed this was to leave behind any negativity and only embrace the positive aspects life offers.

We had come to the full realization that each day should be used and lived to its full potential. As young children Steve and I had to learn not to rely on other people to bring us happiness. Happiness has to come from within. We are glad we have reached that point in our lives and can share it with each other.

With the acceptance we had gained life was easier as we no longer looked for alternative solutions. The tumour and its persistent ongoing symptoms and growth continue to plague Steve. The pain is always there, some days more, some days less but always relentless. He has learned to simply "live" with it. I have learned not to "fight it". We have both learned that acceptance is the key.

Steve and I dance the dance of life and we smile very often. Life is magical and so good.

"The sun shines after the clouds have blown away. The future is bright."

Tips for the patient from Steve

1. Know your own body. Do what feels right for you regardless of any professional advice you may receive. Get second and even third opinions.

2. Ignore all of the kind advice you will receive from well-intentioned unqualified people. Stick with treatment from a professional you trust after following Step 1 above.

3. Do not over-burden your partner or loved ones by harping on about how bad you feel or how much pain you are in. Remember that they are also living with your tumour and assisting you as much as they can. They are also in pain at seeing what you are going through; don't expect them to take on more. Just thank, appreciate and love them more.

4. Don't seek a cure on the internet. This will just confuse you and cause you to annoy your doctors by suggesting all sorts of things you read.

5. Don't think you and your partner are in this alone. Look around the treatment room at your cancer clinic. There is always someone in a worse state than you. Don't feel sorry for yourself. Feel sorry for that other person, especially children who have not experienced a full life.

6. Always look UP! It's amazing how much you notice when you look up that you would never have seen before. (Bev knows what I mean here, but give it a try).

7. Walk away from anything or anyone who takes away from your joy. Life is too short to put up with fools.
8. Give thanks daily when you open your eyes in the morning. You have one more day to spend with your loved ones.

Tips for Caregivers from Bev

1. Always LISTEN to what the patient says about how he feels or what his needs are regardless of any other advice you may be getting.
2. Do not isolate yourself. The first step is to have a valued support system.
3. Do not own the disease. Take a step back and find time to do normal things you would have done before.
4. Ask questions. Do not just accept what you are being told. Use the 5 W and 1 H questions that begin with Why Where Who What and When and then How?
5. Stay off the internet. Too many conflicting areas of "advice" that will send you in all the wrong directions.
6. Set yourself and your patient small achievable goals.
7. You don't have to be strong all the time, it is ok to cry.
8. Remove yourself from any form of negativity. Others who cannot cope will call you a codependent or a martyr. Do not own their stuff.

9. Most important SMILE. Laughter truly is the best medication.

Caregivers manual by Beverly Carinus is available at Amazon KDP Kindle.

One day someone is going to hug you so tight that all of your broken pieces will stick back together - Dance of the Spirit

Creating awareness

She put her hand to my chest, raised her eyes to mine, and called to my soul...Just give me a chance...Just give me a chance"

- Language of the soul

Rebuildconfidence is a non-profit group dedicated to protecting the rights and improving the lives of children who have been the victims of poverty, trafficking and exploitation worldwide. Our mission, through donations, fund-raising and individual sponsorship programs, is to help provide the basic rights to an education and the prospect of realizing a more productive and happy future for these courageous and inspirational children, rebuilding their trust and confidence in themselves and the world.

We aim to bring to attention and support the many NGO Organizations who have the same goals.

http://www.rebuildconfidence.webs.com

Membership: Beverly Carinus – UNESCO-CID - ADTA

<u>Organizations that rebuildconfidence supports in Cambodia.</u>

<u>**www.comped-cam.org**</u>

www.rebuildconfidence.webs.com supports the efforts of COMPED Phnom Penh Cambodia.

Stealing a Generation: The Cambodian Orphanage Industry
*CONTACT: info@sisha.org

Hello Supporters,

The message is out! We've received a lot of press coverage regarding our work investigating and assisting police in shutting down illegal and abusive orphanages. The Brisbane Times, The Sydney Morning Herald, and The Age, called the orphanage industry in Cambodia "the stealing of a generation."

Orphanages in Cambodia are a lucrative business. The children are the assets.

There are the highlights of the reports:

- Over 70 per cent of the 10,000 children living in Cambodia's estimated 600 orphanages have a parent; although research shows most are portrayed as orphans to capitalise on the goodwill of foreign tourists and volunteers, including thousands of Australians.

- Up to 300 of these centres are operating illegally and flouting a push by government and United Nations agencies for children to be reunited with their parents.
- The managers of several respected Australian-run orphanages are alarmed by the situation and note that the number of orphanages has increased 65 per cent in the past five years, while the number of orphans has reduced dramatically as Cambodia recovers from genocide and an AIDS epidemic.
- There are many reports of cash transactions for children, although it is usually referred to as a donation to the child's family.

Help us continue the fight. We can't walk away from these children. Become their Champion. Become a SISHA Champion. Your small gift of $10-$100 helps to free these children and reunite them with their families.

Sincerely,
Steve Morrish
Executive Director
Copyright © 2012 SISHA,
All rights reserved.
www.Rebuildconfidence.webs.com has printed this article with kind permission.

Steve's tumour.

Steve was diagnosed with a rare inoperable left sided Glomus brain stem tumour: for a time it was thought there were two tumours but it was actually one that had moved through a narrow cavity and come out on the other side so it was a bar bell shape.

As the skull is made of bone, there is a fixed amount of space for the brain to take up. The growing tumour increases pressure inside this fixed space and it causes specific problems due to its location.

Where the brain joins the spinal cord is an area called the brain stem, which controls autonomic body functions. Autonomic functions are those that happen without us thinking about them, such as our heartbeat, breathing, digesting food and circulating blood.

Steve has problems with his breathing and lack of oxygen.

The brain stem is also part of the brain that connects the cerebral hemispheres and cerebellum with the spinal cord. All nerve fibers leaving the brain pass through here and go to the limbs and truck of the body.

Steve has constant body aches and nerve pain.

It also connects the rest of the brain to the spinal cords which runs down the back and neck area.

Steve has unbearable neck and back pain due to this.

The brain stem area is responsible for sending out millions of messages from the brain to the rest of the body because Steve's tumour was growing in this area it sends out "crossed wired messages" causing Steve to experience phantom pains. Along with the pain it causes tingling and burning sensations in different parts of the body for apparently no reason.

In the back part of the brain is an area called the cerebellum, which controls balance and coordination. The tumour's growth in this area is responsible for Steve's imbalance and coordination problems.

The hypothalamus is like your brains inner thermostat. The hypothalamus knows what temperature your body should be (about 98.6f or 37C). If your body is too hot the hypothalamus tells it to sweat. If you're too cold it gets you shivering. Both the shivering and sweating are attempts to get your body temperature back to where it needs to be. Steve's hypothalamus got stuck on making him sweat.

Steve's 5th Cranial nerve is affected by the tumour this is a major sensory nerve to the face. It causes Steve to be extremely sensitive to touch.

The 4th ventricle is affected this connects with the centre of the spinal cord and membranes covering the brain so fluid can circulate around and through the brain and spinal cord. The fluid consists mainly of water with a little protein, glucose, some white cells and hormones. Steve's tumour blocks complete circulation of the fluid and these results in increasing pressure in the brain cavity due to buildup of fluid causing the symptoms of headaches, pain and problems with sight and movements.

The tumour continues to cause the following symptoms:

- Sight problems
- Poor coordination and imbalance
- Uncontrollable movement in the eye
- Sickness
- Neck stiffness
- Dizziness
- Extreme headaches
- Difficulty swallowing
- Difficulty breathing
- Difficulty speaking
- Numbness and weakness
- Vasovagal collapse
- Tremours
- Brain hyperactivity
- Unreal perception of time and space
- Lowered immune system.

About Beverly

Member of UNESCO-CID
Member of ADTA

Dr Judy Wallis

http://www.RADTeach.com
Wow Bev, What an amazing story of love, destiny, and
kismet between you and Steve. So grateful you shared. I love
reading your emails, little slices of life, imaginary, intimate
glimpses into people during profound life changes or daily
routines. If you are not writing a book now you should at
least save all the emails you write to compile later into a
narrative. Your email is as remarkable as you are. You write
so beautifully and from your heart. When we met I felt
so comfortable with you and knew you were special. That
became clearer with each passing minute and now the gift
of more of "you" in the email with your background and
wonderful insights and ideas - true wisdom of the mind and
heart. – Dr Judy Wallis

Stella Yfantidis
Beverly is a warm, generous person with a high level of
integrity and professionalism. Caring and wise, she selflessly

puts her heart and soul into her work bringing great joy and happiness to special needs children and adults. A qualified caregiver of the Highest degree I highly support Beverly's humanitarian endeavors and without hesitation encourage you to do the same.

Grant Clark
Journalist, Children's Author
http://monkeymagicbook.com
Beverly is a caring, insightful and conscientious person whose work highlighting the plight of underprivileged kids in Cambodia and helping them recover from the most traumatic start to life is an example to us all.